DRIVE TO VICTORY

Incredible true stories from the
FASTEST SPORT IN THE WORLD

First published in Great Britain in 2025 by Wren & Rook

ISBN: 978 1 5263 6705 1

SRD

Wren & Rook
An imprint of
Hachette Children's Group
Part of Hodder & Stoughton
Carmelite House
50 Victoria Embankment
London EC4Y 0DZ

The authorised representative in the EEA is Hachette Ireland, 8 Castlecourt Centre,
Dublin 15, D15 XTP3, Ireland (email: info@hbgi.ie).

An Hachette UK Company
www.hachette.co.uk
www.hachettechildrens.co.uk

Printed and bound in India by Manipal Technologies Limited, Manipal

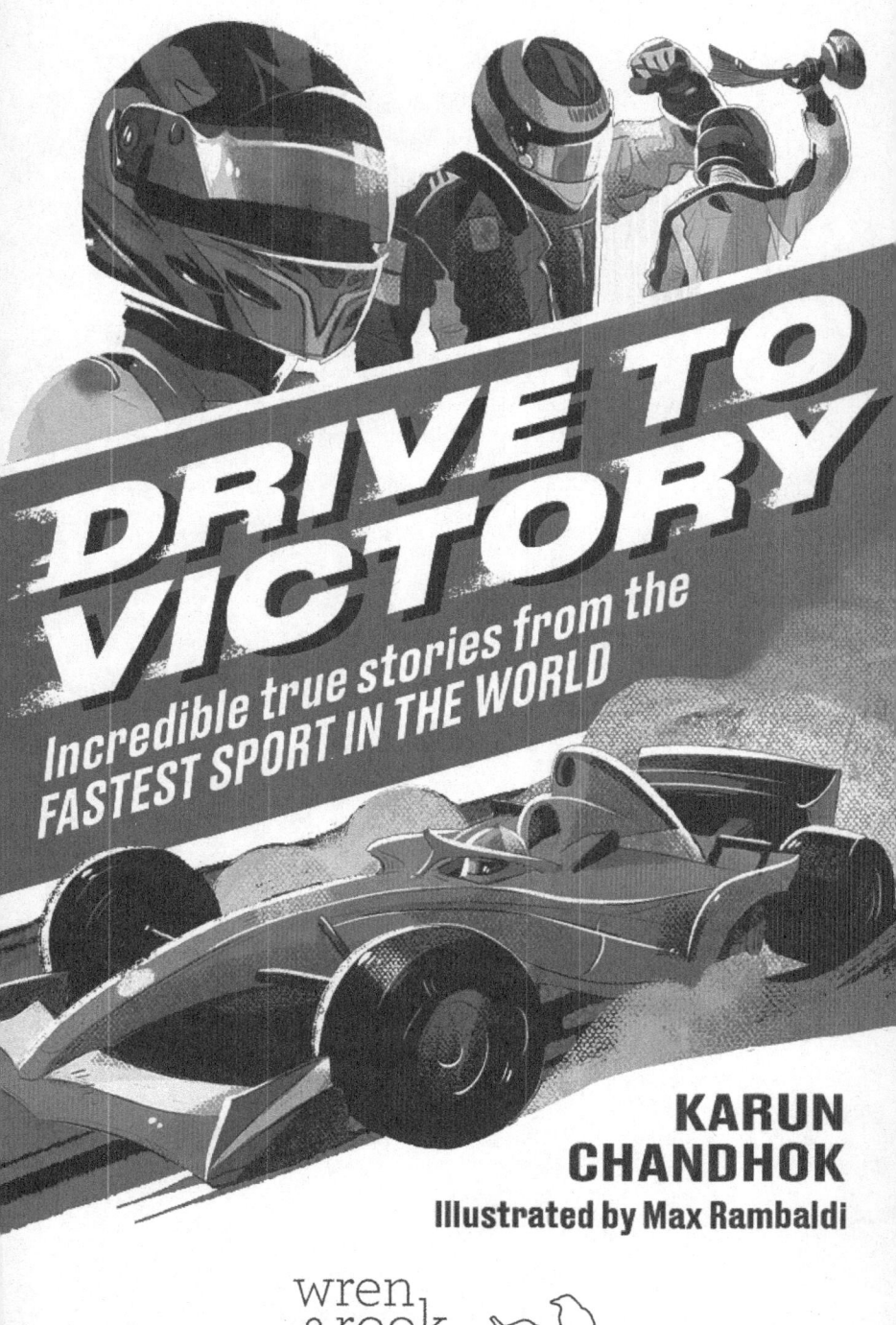

DRIVE TO VICTORY

Incredible true stories from the
FASTEST SPORT IN THE WORLD

**KARUN
CHANDHOK**

Illustrated by Max Rambaldi

wren
&rook

To my parents, who let me follow my dream,
and my children, who inspired me to tell more
kids about the wonderful world of F1.

CONTENTS

INTRODUCTION

I have always been obsessed with motor racing, and when I was a kid, I read as much as I possibly could about Formula 1 racing. I was lucky enough to turn my hobby into a career and was a professional racing car driver for seventeen years, racing all around the world and even in a twenty-four-hour race called the 24 Hours of Le Mans. When I finished racing, I decided to talk about it for a living and now I spend every race weekend commentating on and writing about the sport. It's awesome!

I know just how fun motor racing is to watch too, and I was inspired to write this book after the many weekends I spent watching the races with my own children. My kids ask me all sorts of questions about the drivers, their cars, the tyres and the racetracks, and it made me realise that Formula 1 racing can be a pretty complicated sport and it's hard to understand it when you first start watching it. Someone needed to write a book explaining how it all works and everything there is to know about the drivers and the teams.

Hey! That someone could be me!

So I got writing and now I've written a whole book, and after reading it, you'll know all the important things there are to know about the fastest sport in the world. In these pages, I'll tell you all about the star drivers on the track today and some of the great ones from the past; the top teams and how they got started; how racetracks are actually built; and most importantly, what makes a racing car go really fast!

I hope you enjoy all these incredible stories from the world of racing, and who knows, maybe I'll see YOU on the track some day!

CHAPTER ONE

LIFE IN THE FAST LANE

WHAT IS IT LIKE TO DRIVE REALLY FAST?

What you probably want to know is: how does it feel to be whizzing around a track at 350 kilometres per hour? **That's fast. REALLY FAST!** It's three times as fast as the top speed limit in the UK.

When you first start as a racing car driver, you drive go-karts. Then, if you can handle it, you work your way up the Formula 4, 3 and 2 pyramid by winning races and maybe championships. Then if you're successful, you might get signed by an F1 team as a test driver. And once you're on the team, with hard work and a little bit of luck, you get to take that final step to Formula 1 racing.

As you rise through the car-racing ranks, the cars get faster and faster, so when you do become a Formula 1 driver,

your brain is already used to adapting and adjusting to the increases in speed. That's right: you couldn't just start off as a Formula 1 driver, because your brain wouldn't be ready to react to that kind of speed!

So how does it feel? To me, it's incredibly special. Once you put your foot on the accelerator and turn through a high-speed bend, then you get to feel the full force of Formula 1 racing. **F1 cars will go from 0 to 100 kilometres per hour in just over two seconds,** and more impressively, 200 kilometres per hour in four and a half seconds. You might not think that's very fast, but if you compare it to a high-performance road car like a Porsche 911, which takes ten seconds to get to that same speed, you realise just how fast that is!

I've been very lucky to have driven Formula 1 cars from every decade since the 1930s. The early cars could drive quite fast in a straight line but not very fast on corners in the road. But that all changed in the 1970s as car engineers developed a way for

them to drive round the corners much faster. When you first drive through a corner at high speed it feels like you are about to slide off the track and that can be scary, but all experienced drivers know how to control their cars and stay on the track.

The feeling you get in your stomach when driving through fast corners is the same as when a rollercoaster starts going steeply downhill – your stomach drops and then you get a buzz in the pit of your stomach that fills you with excitement! After that, your competitive instincts kick in, and all you'll want to do is go faster and faster. That's what it feels like taking every corner of a Formula 1 race!

WHAT DOES IT DO TO YOUR BODY?

When I first told my parents that I wanted to be a racing driver, their first piece of advice wasn't to learn to drive a car but to get fit! Like many teenagers, exercise was not my favourite thing and I often ate unhealthily, so it took me ten months to get fit enough to endure the g-forces of a racing car.

Hold on, you're probably thinking, **why do racing drivers need to be fit?** People sometimes think that racing drivers just sit in a car and drive round and round in circles – it's not exactly a workout, is it?! Well, imagine you're driving a car along a twisty country lane. You're moving around in your seat, and it takes a bit of effort to stay upright. That's because there is a gravitational force, or g-force, pushing your body in the opposite direction to where the car is taking you.

Now imagine if you were going around that same corner with **TEN TIMES** the g-force pushing you over. It would take a lot of energy to stay upright, wouldn't it? You'd have to use your body to push back against the g-force. That's what happens in a Formula 1 car for the whole two hours of a Grand Prix (that's what we call the race). The drivers' heads and necks are especially affected by the g-force because they're poking out of the top of the car, so they have to be really strong.

Want to experience g-force at home?

Try lying on your back, with your shoulders at the end of the bed and your head hanging off the end. Now try and hold it upright off the end of the bed for one minute. It's hard, isn't it?! (Make sure you hold on to the bed frame to stop you from falling off!)

Imagine the drivers having to do that for two hours whilst wearing a heavy helmet! And that's just one thing that drivers have to be able to do. They also need to have super stamina to perform at their best for a two-hour Grand Prix and be able to handle the shocks going through their spine as they sit just 2 centimetres off the ground. And, if that wasn't tiring enough, it's very hot in the car – sometimes over 50 degrees Celsius – and the drivers are sitting in fireproof race suits that are made of a thick material, which means they end up sweating out as much as 3 litres of fluid in a hot race. It's a sweaty sport!

Racing drivers also need to have strong legs. Did you know that when the drivers press the brake pedal, they need to apply a huge amount of pressure because the brakes are made out of carbon, which only works properly when heated up above 400 degrees Celsius?! Most road cars have steel brakes, so you only need to press the pedal lightly. Imagine if you were going down a steep hill on your bicycle and tried to stop just by using the muscles in one leg instead of using your brakes. Pretty

tough, right? Now imagine doing that at every corner of every lap of a Formula 1 race – that's what the drivers need to do!

You're probably thinking, *Wow, that all sounds exhausting!* It is! But racing drivers train their bodies and their minds to be resilient and they have teams of people helping them with their fitness, nutrition and everything else it takes to be a successful athlete. The good news is that the drivers are free to pick any form of workout they like to keep them fit, from cycling to running or even cross-country skiing! When I raced, I used to keep fit by playing squash. Except I would use a hexagon-shaped ball instead of a round ball and I'd throw it against the squash court's walls. Because of the weird shape, it would bounce back in an unpredictable way, so trying to catch it would be really good for keeping my reflexes sharp.

You have to be very committed to training your body to be a racing driver, but the thrill of the race is definitely worth it!

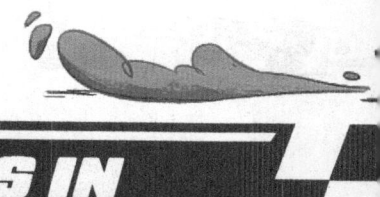

DRIVING IS IN MY DNA!

Now you know what it's like to sit behind the wheel, let's rewind to how I became a professional racing-car driver. I grew up dreaming of being a Formula 1 driver. I loved watching the cars flying around the track at high speed and I would think to myself, *Wow, that's what I want to do when I grow up.*

I was lucky to achieve my dream, especially because I've become **one of only TWO Indian racing-car drivers so far** to have competed in Formula 1 races. Out of the 1,300,000,000 Indians on earth, only myself and Narain Karthikeyan have made it on to the F1 grid, which is a pretty exclusive club – maybe we should get membership cards! I am also the only Indian who's raced in all the top three categories of the Fédération Internationale de l'Automobile's (FIA's) global motorsport (this is the sports federation that looks after all motorsports).

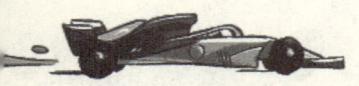

I have raced in Formula 1 events, the World Endurance Championship (which involves long distance races between six and twenty-four hours long) and Formula E, the first ever electric-powered World Championship.

So, how did I get there? I was born in India in 1984 into a car-crazy, motorsport-loving family. When India got independence

from British rule in 1947, there were several airfields around the country that were made into makeshift motor-racing tracks. My grandfather, Indu, is known as the godfather of Indian motorsport, because together with his friends he used to organise races for amateur drivers. This was so popular that my grandfather created the Madras Motor Sports Club, which raised money to build the first ever racetrack in India, on the outskirts of Madras (now re-named Chennai), where our family are from. The Madras Motor Racing Track opened in 1990, and in 2024 I took my son to drive around it in a go-kart. So we now have had four generations of our family drive around the same track!

My grandad wasn't the only family member who loved to race – I had a racing grandmother too! My grandmother, Indra, loved motor racing and even began competing herself in the 1970s. This is especially amazing because at that time in India, it really wasn't common for women to be driving on the road, let alone in a race. She would often tell me the story of how the

door of her car once flew open and she drove the rest of the race holding the door with one hand, steering with the other, and still finished third ... Good going, Granny!

Despite having the godfather of Indian motorsport for a grandfather and an awe-inspiring driver for a grandmother, it was my dad who had the biggest influence on me. As a child, I spent every weekend travelling with him to the racetrack, often watching him compete. He used to race in Formula 2 and Formula 3 cars, and also took part in rallies. Rallies often take place on dirt roads and, unlike in formula racing when the cars all set off together, the cars go out one by one. He became my manager when I started racing and then he worked on bringing Formula 1 racing to India, which he finally managed in 2011. So it's definitely in my DNA to live life in the fast lane!

Do you think you could be a Formula 1 driver?

CHAPTER TWO

UNDER THE BONNET

Before we get into who the drivers and teams are, let's get to know a little bit more about the sport.

In this chapter, you will learn about how the sport became the amazing championship that it is today, what it takes to organise a race weekend, what exactly happens in a pit stop and how racing cars are made. I'll also tell you about the technology that makes the cars so sleek and fast, and I'll get you up to speed with all the lingo we F1 fans use.

THE BASICS

The Formula 1 World Championship takes place in five continents – Europe, Asia, North America, South America and Oceania. Currently, ten teams compete and each team has two drivers, so the race consists of twenty drivers in total. These athletes push themselves mentally and physically to the limit to drive at over 350 kilometres per hour around twisty, high-speed tracks.

The teams and drivers compete in around twenty-five Grands Prix per year, with the top ten finishers in every race scoring points. These points are then added up throughout the season, at the end of which the team and driver with the most points are crowned the World Drivers' Champion or World Constructors' Champion. This is when they win the big prize money pots as well!

FORMULA FACT

Every team has to make their own car, with thousands of parts designed and built for their car and their car alone.

As of 2026, there will be five different engines in the sport, with some of them supplying more than one team. The teams are made up of huge groups of around 1,000 people who do all sorts of different jobs from building the cars to working in the catering department. Imagine that – 1,000 people just to build two cars that go racing around a track. Pretty crazy, right?!

THE MAN WHO HELPED FORMULA 1 RACING GET SO BIG

So where did it all begin? F1 races started in the 1920s, but the first ever proper World Championship race was the British Grand Prix, held way back in 1950. It was such a big day that even the King of England went to watch! F1 races were held in different parts of the world, but they weren't organised particularly well and more importantly, people at home couldn't always watch them on TV either. Do you want to know how F1 racing exploded into this amazing spectacle that you can see from your living room?

The answer to that is really down to one man – Bernie Ecclestone. Bernie had always been a fan of motor racing. He wasn't a good enough driver to be a top racer, but he did have a good eye for business and took over a Formula 1 team called Brabham in the 1970s.

He was a great team principal (a team leader is called a team principal) and led the team to become world champions in 1981 and 1983.

But Bernie soon realised that Formula 1 racing could be much bigger than it was if someone dedicated their time into making it a professional sport. So Bernie sold his team and became the head of the Formula One Constructors' Association, whose job was to promote the sport. He worked really hard, signing deals with racetracks around the world and most TV channels, so that by the early 1990s, Formula 1 races were shown across the world to millions of people. They are now watched by 80 million people every race! Bernie also realised that the safety standards in the sport needed to improve and hired a doctor called Sid Watkins to set up a top medical team at every race in the 1980s.

Without Bernie's help, Formula 1 racing wouldn't be the sport it is today.

THE F1 WORLD CHAMPIONSHIP

Unlike some other sports, we don't have loads of fixtures. There used to be fewer than ten races each championship season, but now we're up to twenty-four races per year. We race in the Formula 1 World Championship from March to December.

In each race, the drivers score points depending on what order they finish in. The points from each race get added up and at the end of the year, the total number of points they get determines their finishing position in the Drivers' World Championship. The teams also score points in the Constructors' World Championship. Winning the Constructors' World Championship is based on the amount of points the team have scored throughout the season. This is the total number of points scored by both the cars in the team added

together. The tricky bit is that although there are usually twenty drivers competing in each race, only the top ten score points. You don't want to come in eleventh!

FORMULA FACT

The first official Drivers' World Championship was in 1950, and Italian driver Giuseppe Farina won it.

The first Constructors' World Championship was eight years later in 1958, and the British team Vanwall won it.

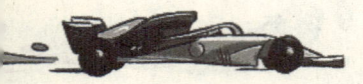

So why is the Constructors' World Championship so important? Of course, it's brilliant when a team's driver wins lots of races, but to stay in the top position, the team need lots of money. The higher the team finishes in the Constructors' World Championship, the more prize money they get. Every position is worth millions of dollars, which they can use to upgrade the car or buy new equipment, keeping them at the top of their game.

WHAT HAPPENS ON RACE WEEKEND?

Well, first off, it's not actually a weekend! A race weekend is three days long, starting with practice sessions on the Friday, then the Qualifying session on Saturday, which determines the starting order for the race on Sunday. Plus, in 2021, an extra short race called the Sprint was introduced. These only happen six times a year and, on these weekends, the teams have just one practice session and then do a short race which is about a third of the distance of the main Grand Prix. In this race, the drivers score points based on where they come in the race. First place is eight points and then you get one point less with every place that you go down the rankings.

Before the big race, the drivers spend time in a simulator. This is like a super high-tech video game warm-up! We practise driving round a computerised version of the real track. We

37

won't always have driven on the racetrack before, so we want to learn the corners before the real race.

Imagine spending your whole lunch break practising for a race. Now imagine doing that three times over . . . The simulator practice sessions go on for a full eight hours back at the team factories before the drivers get to the tracks and start practising in the real cars. That's pretty tiring for their eyes to be staring at a screen for so long, don't you think?

The practice sessions on track are a good chance for the teams and drivers to get the car set up right for the races. Unlike road cars, F1 cars have 'wings' (which don't look anything like plane wings by the way!). They're part of the body of the car and you have one on the front and one on the back. It's very important to get the right balance between them.

The drivers will always be looking for the right balance to make sure that neither the front nor the back of the car is sliding, because that determines how fast they can take the straights and corners on the track.

Qualifying is a very exciting hour for the drivers. We love it! It's the only time during the weekend where we can really go for it, driving our cars at 100% of their speed and pushing to our absolute limit. It's a very important part of the weekend, because if you start the race from the front, you have a better chance of winning at the end. The Qualifying session is broken up into three parts, with five drivers getting knocked out after the first eighteen minutes. Then five more drivers get knocked out after another fifteen minutes. Finally, ten go into a shootout in the last part, which determines the starting order for the race on Sunday. The driver who is the fastest in Qualifying is rewarded with 'pole position'.

THE RACE IS ON!

Every race is around 300 kilometres, which means it could be anywhere between forty-five and seventy-eight laps of a track, depending how long it is. Forty minutes before the start of the race, the cars all leave their pit garages and head out to the starting grid. The cars have last-minute checks, the teams talk strategy and the drivers do their TV interviews. Then just before the start, the drivers do a formation lap to warm up the brakes and tyres before lining up at the starting grid. Five red lights come on one by one, and when they all go out . . .

5

4

3

2

1

. . . the race is on!

TECH TALK

Driving really fast doesn't just take skill. It also takes a really fast car. Who wins or loses a race is largely to do with how good the car they're driving is. In football or rugby or basketball, the teams all play using the same ball, but in Formula 1 racing, each car is different. Some cars share the same make of engine, as only a few companies make racing engines, but they all have completely different settings on them and each car can be a slightly different shape or size. This can give the drivers an advantage over the competition as teams will customise the car to fit the skillset of its driver. Imagine having a car that was completely personalised to you!

41

HOW DO YOU BUILD A RACING CAR?

You've probably noticed that an F1 car looks nothing like the cars you see on the road. It takes about four years to build a road car, from designing it to testing it on the road. Once the manufacturers start producing a road car, the design doesn't change until they develop a new model, which is often a few years later. But in Formula 1 racing, the cars are rebuilt every single year! And they might even make tweaks to a car after every race to improve its speed and reliability. This means that there is always a team of mechanics and engineers working on the F1 cars throughout the season.

FORMULA FACT

There are 11,000 parts in an F1 car and nearly every one of those parts is uniquely designed just for that car. For example, you can't take a front wing from a Mercedes F1 car and put it on a Ferrari F1 car. It won't fit!

The design of a Formula 1 car is broken up into three main parts – the chassis, engine and gearbox.

THE CHASSIS

This is the spine of the car. It's where the driver sits, and everything else on the car is fitted to the chassis. The petrol tank sits inside the chassis and the driver's seat actually leans against the petrol tank but is protected by carbon fibre. The bodywork and front suspension parts are all bolted to the chassis, which gives the car its shape and allows the front wheels to be in the right position.

COCKPIT

PETROL TANK

THE ENGINE

This is fitted to the back of the chassis. In the 2024 F1 season, there were five different engines in use – Ferrari, Mercedes, Red Bull Powertrains, Renault and Honda. From 2026, Renault will no longer be making engines, while Audi will join the grid.

Since 2014, F1 engines have been hybrids, which means that the cars now have both petrol and electrical power. Along the side of the car, there are parts called radiators and coolers, which help to control the temperature of the water and oil used in the engine.

The average F1 engine creates about 1,000 horsepower. If you compare that to the engine in an average road car, like a Volkswagen Golf, it is about eight times the amount of power!

EXHAUST PIPE

PETROL ENGINE

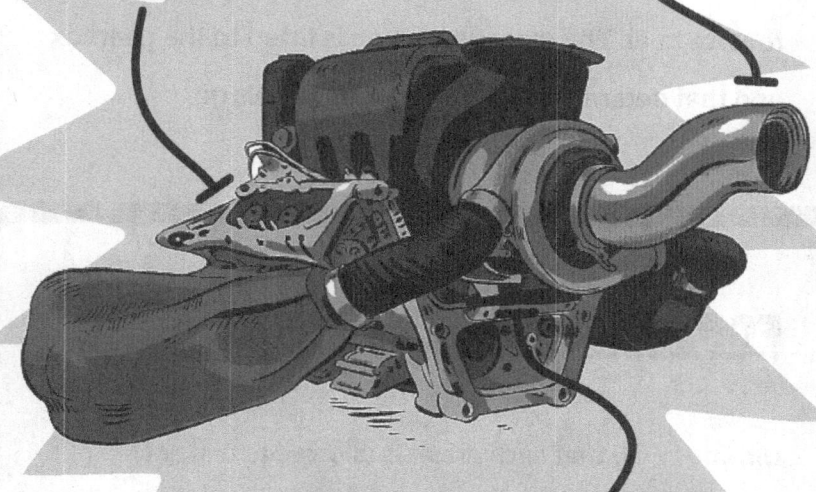

TURBOCHARGER

THE GEARBOX

Behind the engine sits the gearbox. This has nine gears – eight to go forward, which help the car to get the best performance, just like in a road car, and the ninth is a reverse gear. The rear suspension is fitted to the gearbox and that determines where the rear wheels go.

FORMULA FACT

Did you know that each driver is allowed to use only five gearboxes throughout the whole F1 season? They need to be really careful not to break them in a crash!

GEARBOX OUTER CASING

GEAR CLUSTERS

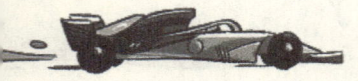

But how do you start to build an F1 car? The first step is all down to the design team. They think about every part of the car and how they all connect together. They draw their designs on computers and once they're happy, they make a scale model, which is 60% of the size of the real car. They put this model car in a wind tunnel to better understand how their car will react on the track and to see if they've got the design right.

Once the car is designed, it's sent to the manufacturing department, who make the parts. These are made mainly out of carbon fibre, which is super strong but also very light. It's very important to have cars that are not heavy because any extra weight makes them slower.

Once the parts are made, they are all sent to be inspected to see if they can withstand g-force and vibrations out on the track. If every part passes, then they are sent to the race bays where the mechanics put the car together. This step is kind of like assembling a massive LEGO® set, except that you get a real racing car at the end of it!

BOX! BOX!

Have you heard the teams say 'box, box' and wondered what it means? When a team says 'box, box', they are telling their driver to go in for a pit stop. This is where the drivers come off the track into the pit lane and their team change their tyres or try to quickly fix some damaged parts.

In the pit lane, there are three people working at every corner of the car – one takes the old tyre off, one puts the new tyre on and the third uses the 'wheel gun' to loosen and tighten the wheels. There are two people known as jackmen who lift up the front and back of the car, two people to hold the car steady, two people to adjust the front wing angle and one person who keeps an eye on the traffic in the pit lane to send the car back out.

There will also be a few more mechanics with spare jacks, wheel guns or wheel nuts just in case there are any issues during the pit stop.

It's very important for the driver to stop in exactly the right spot so the mechanics can do a really fast pit stop. If it all goes perfectly, they can change all four tyres and send the car back out in **less than two seconds!**

There have been times in the past when F1 cars also used to get a top-up of petrol during their pit stops. The fuel rig used to pump in 12 litres of fuel every second – imagine if you could fill up your family car at the petrol station in just five seconds! But this was also quite dangerous for the mechanics as the leaking fuel could cause a fire, so now all the cars start the race with enough petrol to get them to the end of the race.

IT'S ALL ABOUT THE AERODYNAMICS

To put it simply, aerodynamics just means the way the air flows over and under a race car, as well as how the air flow gets thrown away from the car as it passes along the track. When the air flows over and under the car, it produces something known as downforce, which pushes the car into the ground. The more downforce you have, the faster you can go round the corners. So aerodynamics is a very important part of winning F1 races.

FORMULA FACT

Formula 1 cars produce so much downforce that if they drove into a tunnel at full speed, they could create enough momentum to drive upside down on the ceiling!

How cool is that?

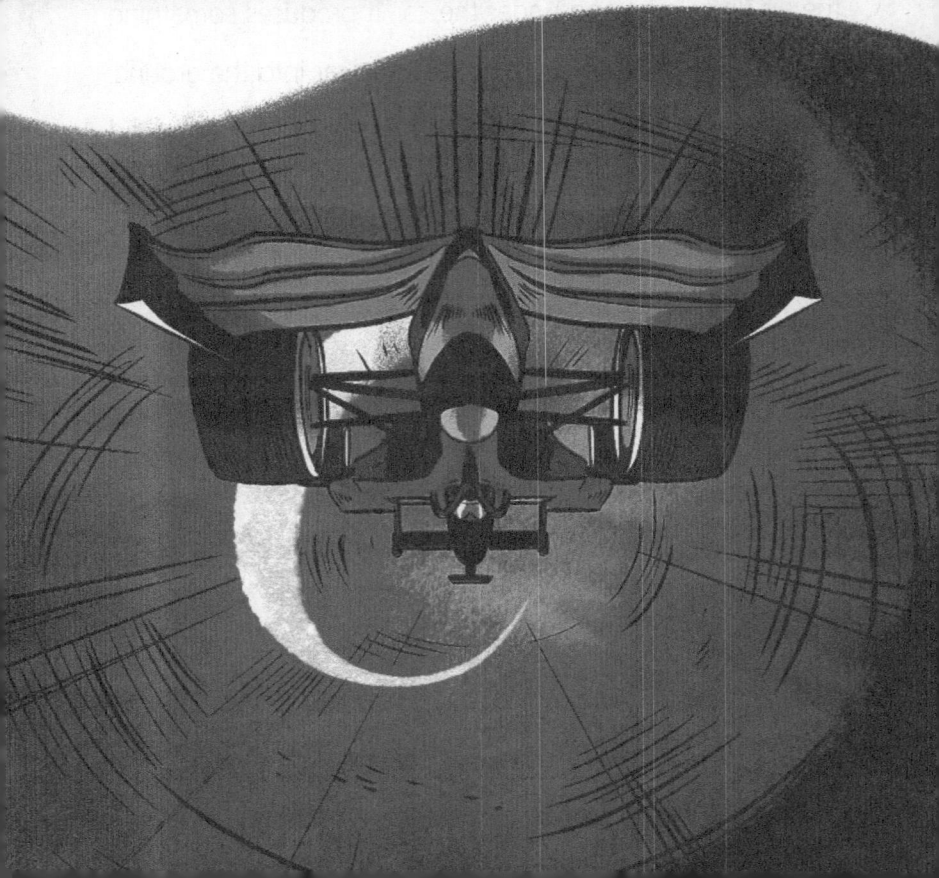

This air flow also produces something called drag, which is a measure of how much a car is being slowed down by the air flow. When you drive down the straights, you want as little drag as possible so you can go really fast.

One of the big challenges is that a lot of downforce also creates a lot of drag. So if you have a car with lots of downforce, you'll be really fast in the corners but slow on the straights. This is why the teams have to find the right balance of downforce and drag so their cars can be fast on the straights and also in the corners.

To help with this, F1 cars have wings. No, not like the wings on a plane. The wings on a plane are designed to help lift the plane up into the sky, but the wings on an F1 car are designed to push the car down to the ground and create downforce.

The front wing helps to give the car more front grip and the rear wing helps to control the rear of the car. F1 cars started

having wings in the 1960s and they have become more and more complex over time. Now they look like pieces of art!

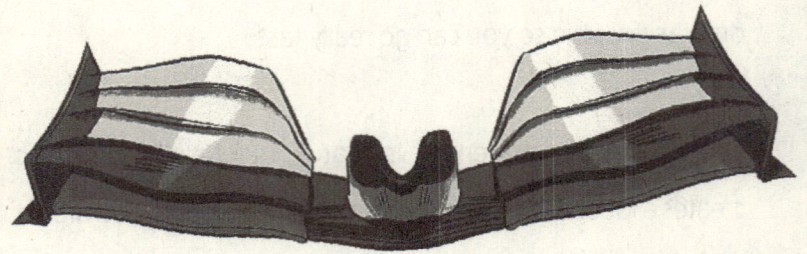

In the late 1970s, designers also realised that the bottom of the car, known as the floor, can help to produce a lot of downforce. This was a very important discovery because they realised that this downforce created very little drag and so only slowed the cars down a little bit on the straights. This made the cars a lot faster through the corners but nearly as fast when going straight, which is a real bonus. Nowadays, over half the downforce produced by the cars comes from the performance of the floor, so it's a really critical part to get right.

YOU'VE GOT TO HAVE GRIP

So we know that F1 cars are contending with aerodynamics, super-powerful engines and wings, but what helps them stay on the track? The tyres! Tyres are a really important part of a Formula 1 car because they are the only four parts of a car which connect the other 11,000 parts to the road. If the tyres are not good or not working properly, then the whole car doesn't work properly.

Unlike the tyres you see on road cars, when the track is dry, Formula 1 cars use tyres called slicks with no tread lines on them. That means that there is more rubber in contact with the road and it gives them more grip. When you watch F1 racing, you'll notice that the tyres can have different coloured stripes on their sides. That's because there are three different types of tyres.

SOFT TYRES – with a red stripe: The soft tyres offer the most amount of grip and are the fastest, but they will wear out more quickly than the others.

MEDIUM TYRES – with a yellow stripe: Harder than the soft tyre but not as hard as the hard tyres. These ones are good for durability (speed and staying on the track).

HARD TYRES – with a white stripe: The hard tyres are the ones that will last the longest but they're the slowest, so it can be risky to use these tyres as other people may overtake you.

Throughout a race weekend, you will see the drivers using all these different tyres when the weather is dry. The teams only have a few of each tyre to use over the weekend, so they have to plan very wisely to decide which ones to use and when.

The race rules also say that they have to use a minimum of two different types of tyres during the race, so choosing when to switch is a really important part of the strategy.

When it rains, the drivers have two different options:

INTERMEDIATE TYRES – with a green stripe: Used when there's a light drizzle or a lightly damp track.

WET TYRES – with a blue stripe: Used when there is heavy rain and a lot of water on the track.

FORMULA FACT

The full wet tyre can shift 85 litres of water every second when the car is doing 300 kilometres per hour, which means it can empty a full bathtub every one and a half seconds!

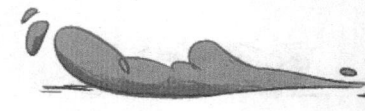

Wow, there's a lot that goes into making and driving a Formula 1 car. But there's one more part of the car that we haven't talked about yet, which is SUPER important! That's right: the steering wheel.

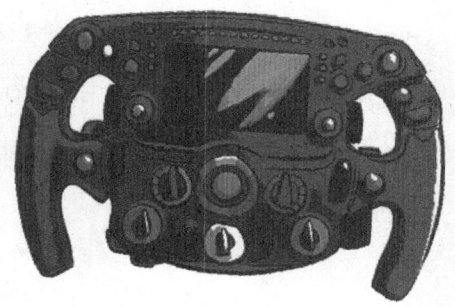

F1 steering wheels have over twenty-five different buttons and switches, plus paddles to change gears and a clutch paddle. That's more buttons than a video game controller! Every team has their own bespoke steering wheel, and the drivers can also pick where the buttons go on the steering wheel to suit their grip. They have LED lights, often in different colours, which tell them when it's time to change

gear, and they also have a screen on the steering wheel which tells them their lap times, the amount of battery power in their hybrid system and the temperature of their tyres and engine.

The brakes and the gearbox on a Formula 1 car are both controlled by electronics, so the drivers are able to change their settings using the buttons on the steering wheel. For example, when they press the brake pedal with their foot, they can adjust just how much of the brake pressure is applied to the front brakes of the car and how much is applied to the back brakes. This can help them stabilise the car when driving through a corner.

The drivers can also choose different modes depending on how much power they get from the electric motors and batteries. Just like any of your toys, if they run at full power all the time, the batteries won't last for too long and the engines themselves will start to have issues. So the teams keep a careful eye and count every single kilometre that is run in

every single engine mode so that they can switch between them and make sure the engines and batteries last for the whole race.

Now that you know a bit more about how the cars are built and work, **would you like to work in an F1 team one day?** The drivers get all the glory and the fans celebrate them, but without the amazing team of people designing and building their cars, they would have no chance of winning!

The teams are made up of many people, including designers and engineers looking at the wings, floor and bodywork, the suspension and tyres as well as the engines and all the cooling systems. They have people looking at the colour schemes and marketing ideas, because without the money from sponsors, they wouldn't be able to build the cars. They also have lawyers, accountants, chefs, doctors and psychologists. So if you love Formula 1 racing, there are so many ways to be a part of the team!

CHAPTER THREE

THE FASTEST DRIVERS IN THE WORLD

Now that we've learnt about the way Formula 1 events work and how the cars are built, it's time to find out a bit more about the stars of the show — the drivers! There are twenty amazing drivers on the grid today, but do you know how they made it to F1 racing and what makes them special? Let's take a look at some of them . . .

SIR LEWIS HAMILTON

The biggest star on the Formula 1 grid. By 2024, Lewis had won seven world championships and held the record for the highest number of race victories and pole positions in the sport. So how did he become one of the greatest drivers in the world?

When he was just eight years old, Lewis went to the McLaren team boss Ron Dennis and asked for an autograph. He told Ron that he dreamt of driving for McLaren's F1 team one day and amazingly Ron kept an eye out for him before signing him up. McLaren took Lewis under their wing and guided him from go-karts to becoming an F1 driver.

Lewis became the Formula Renault champion (an entry level motor race that no longer exists) when he was eighteen, and

shortly after, he became the Formula 3 champion and the 2006 GP2 champion (GP2 is what Formula 2 racing used to be called), before starting his first F1 season at the beginning of 2007. This would go down in history as the greatest season by a rookie driver so far. He finished on the podium in his first nine races and was a contender for the world championship right until the final race. Despite being teammates with Fernando Alonso, who was already a double world champion, he ended up losing the championship by just one point to Kimi Räikkönen and equal on points with Alonso in his debut season. That's an impressive start!

The following season, Lewis bounced back to win the title in the most dramatic finish ever against Ferrari's Felipe Massa, becoming world champion for the first time. At the title decider on Massa's home turf in Brazil, Lewis claimed fifth place and the four points he needed to become champion on the final corner of the final lap of the final race! Lewis stayed with the McLaren team for another four seasons until the end of 2012,

when he shocked the Formula 1 world by choosing to leave McLaren to join the Mercedes team, who at that time were the fourth best Formula 1 team, while McLaren was second.

It was a risky move but ended up being the best thing that could have happened to Lewis's career. Lewis went on to win six more world championships with Mercedes – a record that equals F1 legend Michael Schumacher.

But the Mercedes dream had to come to an end, and after two less successful seasons in 2022 and 2023, Lewis shocked the motor racing world again by announcing he was leaving Mercedes and joining their big rivals at Ferrari for the 2025 season. This was one of the most surprising team swaps in F1 history, but if we've learnt anything from Lewis's last team change, this can only mean more world titles!

Not only is Lewis a record-breaking driver; he is also the only Black driver to have ever raced in Formula 1 events, and he

created the Mission 44 foundation to encourage educational programmes around the world to help more young people get involved in the sport, no matter what their background.

BEST EVER RACE

It was a very wet day at the 2008 British Grand Prix and after starting in fourth place on the grid, Lewis stormed up into the lead and was off. The other drivers didn't have a chance at catching up with him. He finished an incredible sixty-eight seconds in front of everyone else!

74

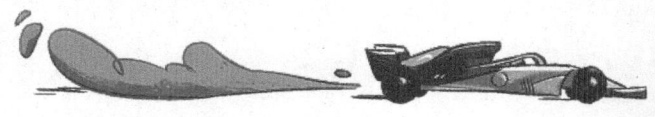

MAX VERSTAPPEN

Max Verstappen is a racing phenomenon! By twenty-seven he had already won his fourth world championship and he is considered to be one of the most talented F1 drivers ever.

His father, Jos, was a Formula 1 driver and started training Max in go-karts when he was four years old. They spent many hours together at the go-kart track and Jos guided his son up the car-racing ladder. Jos took Max to the track in all sorts of weather conditions to help him develop his skills and coached him on the best way to race wheel-to-wheel with his rivals.

Max did just one Formula 3 season before he was picked up by the Red Bull driver programme and placed with their junior team, Toro Rosso. After just one and a half seasons at Toro Rosso, Max was promoted to the main Red Bull Racing team.

At only eighteen years old, Max won his very first race with Red Bull in Barcelona in 2016. He became the youngest ever F1 race winner and is the first driver from Holland to win a Grand Prix and become world champion.

In 2021, Max and Lewis fought a season-long battle and arrived at the final race equal on points (read more about this in chapter six). Max overtook Lewis on the final lap of the whole year and ended up becoming the youngest ever F1 world champion when he was just twenty-four years old. He went on to dominate the sport for the next two seasons, racking up over fifty race victories.

But Max isn't just a star on the grid. In fact, he's also an excellent esports player, having played racing games online since he was a child. He likes nothing better than going home from a long day of racing to a long evening of online racing! He loves it so much that he even brings his racing games with him on the plane when he's travelling to races.

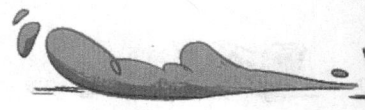

BEST EVER RACE

Max's potential as a future world champion was proven in the 2016 Brazilian Grand Prix, when he finished third after being in sixteenth place for some of the race. He flew past the opposition to score a podium place on a perilously wet day at the Interlagos track.

77

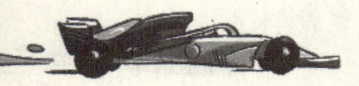

LANDO NORRIS

Lando Norris has quickly become the next British golden boy, after joining the McLaren team in 2018. His cheeky and funny personality has drawn a lot of young fans to the sport and his speed has made his rivals sit up and take notice.

Lando began racing go-karts at a very young age and went on to become the youngest ever world karting champion at the age of just fourteen. His childhood hero was the motorcycle racing legend Valentino Rossi, and Lando's neon yellow helmet is inspired by Valentino's own helmet designs.

Lando became a Formula 4 champion and both a Formula 3 and Formula 2 race winner, competing alongside George Russell and Alex Albon in the junior categories.

The three of them continue to be very good friends today while they compete together in Formula 1 races.

After graduating from F2 racing, Lando was a test driver for the McLaren team and got promoted to the race seat in 2019. Did you know that Lando came very close to winning his first race in Russia in 2021? He was leading the entire race until it rained near the end, but he didn't change to wet tyres and ended up sliding off the track! Lando had to wait almost three years, but on a glorious sunny day in Miami he drove a brilliant race to finally win his first Grand Prix, and has since then grown in confidence to take more victories, which made him a championship contender in 2024.

Like Max Verstappen, Lando is also a big gamer and has his own esports team called Quadrant, with which he competes in different gaming competitions. If you play games online, you might one day find yourself playing against him!

BEST EVER RACE

At the Dutch Grand Prix in 2024, Norris was absolutely unstoppable. After taking a commanding pole position, he was beaten at the start by Max Verstappen. Despite the home crowd cheering for Max, Lando roared past him and then scampered away to win the race by a whopping twenty-two seconds.

GEORGE RUSSELL

A cool, calm, perfectionist, George Russell is quickly becoming an F1 star. He was a F4, GP3 and F2 champion before joining the Williams Formula 1 team in 2019.

The English driver is one of the fastest drivers in Formula 1 Qualifying at the moment, and despite the Williams team going through a tough period where their car was often at the back of the pack, Russell put in some very strong performances for the team.

After a one-off appearance in 2020, George was rewarded with a contract to join Lewis Hamilton at Mercedes for the 2022 season and made an immediate impact by challenging his seven-time World Championship-winning teammate.

Russell won his first ever race in Brazil later that year and finished his hugely impressive first season with the team ahead of Hamilton in the World Championship ranking.

In his time in F1 racing, Russell has gained a reputation for being one of the hardest working drivers on the grid and is also a driver who constantly seeks to improve the sport.

He is a director of the Grand Prix Drivers' Association and often leads the way when it comes to speaking to the officials in charge of the F1 Championship to make the changes that the drivers want.

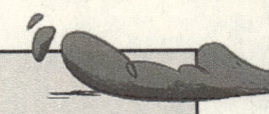

BEST EVER RACE

In 2020, Lewis Hamilton was ill and missed the Sakhir Grand Prix held in Bahrain. Mercedes drafted in George Russell to replace him and he absolutely stunned the F1 world by qualifying in second place. He took the lead early on and was all set for a sensational victory on his Mercedes debut until a puncture with just ten laps to go ruined his day. It was a phenomenal performance that assured him a future Mercedes seat.

84

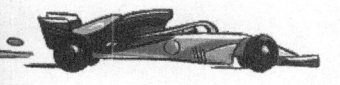

CHARLES LECLERC

Born in the lavish town of Monaco, racer Charles Leclerc is one of the most popular drivers on the grid. He was signed by Ferrari as a junior Formula 1 driver and has risen up the ranks to join the Ferrari Formula 1 team.

Charles is incredibly fast and arguably one of the best qualifiers on the F1 grid. He has an amazing ability to extract the maximum performance from the car for that one magic lap in Qualifying, and by the summer of 2024 had already racked up twenty-five pole positions alongside his seven victories, including a fairy-tale win at Monaco. How cool is it that he won a Formula 1 race on the same streets that he rode his bike to school on when he was a kid?

He made his debut with the Sauber team in 2018 and finished with four times as many points as his more experienced teammate, Marcus Ericsson. It was clear Charles was a special talent.

Ferrari promoted him up to their main race team for the 2019 season, giving Leclerc a chance to drive alongside four-time world champion Sebastian Vettel in the iconic red Ferrari cars. He surprised everyone by finishing ahead of Vettel in their next two seasons together, scoring the first two wins of his career in Belgium and Italy in 2019.

By 2022, Charles was the closest challenger to Max Verstappen for the World Championship. He fought a tough campaign, winning three races and taking nine pole positions, but was ultimately beaten and ended the year with a career best of second place.

When he's not racing, Charles is playing chess. In fact, he's a very good chess player and is often found playing games on the plane on his way to the races. He has a younger brother, Arthur Leclerc, who is also a racing driver and has been a Formula 2 race winner. That's one fast family!

BEST EVER RACE

At the Italian Grand Prix in 2019, Leclerc had an emotional victory in front of the adoring Ferrari fans who had gathered to watch him. After starting on pole position, Leclerc came under attack from both the Mercedes drivers, Lewis Hamilton and Valtteri Bottas, but he kept his cool and drove to victory, sending the crowd wild!

FERNANDO ALONSO

Fernando Alonso is one of the greatest racing drivers that the sport has ever seen. He started racing in 2001 and is still fast and hungry for success despite now being one of the oldest drivers on the grid (he's in his forties). Fernando has taken over 100 podium finishes and is the only driver in the history of the sport to have competed in over 400 races!

Alonso began his career with the Minardi team, a small Italian team that didn't have a lot of money or fast cars. Yet somehow, Fernando managed to muscle his way up the ranks and earn himself a spot on the Renault Formula 1 team. He won his first race in 2003 and became a double world champion in 2005 and 2006. He then left Renault to join the McLaren team in 2007. After a dramatic season where he lost the championship by just one point, he left the team to go back to Renault in 2008.

Alonso has also raced for Ferrari, and in his time with them he twice came very close to becoming world champion, in both 2010 and 2012. In fact, Fernando is only eight points away from being a five-time world champion! After an unsuccessful season with the McLaren team in 2015, Alonso decided to take a break from the F1 world. The two biggest non-F1 races are the Indianapolis 500 and the 24 Hours of Le Mans, and Fernando decided to try and win those instead. He won the Le Mans race twice, but sadly his engine failed when he was fighting with the leaders at Indianapolis.

He returned to F1 racing in 2021 with the Alpine team (formerly called Renault) and then switched to Aston Martin Racing for 2023. The Spaniard is one of the smartest F1 drivers ever to race and is often heard making clever strategy calls about his race despite driving around at over 300 kilometres per hour! He is also an excellent driver in wheel-to-wheel combat, which means he's often able to position his car in ways that help him sneak past his rivals.

BEST EVER RACE

At the European Grand Prix on the streets of Valencia in 2012, Alonso won the race with an awe-inspiring performance. Starting down in eleventh place, Alonso jumped up to eighth on the opening lap and soon unleashed some amazing speed that helped him work his way up to the front position. Seeing him win that race in front of his home crowd was really emotional for everyone in Spain!

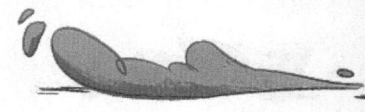

CARLOS SAINZ JUNIOR

Williams driver Carlos Sainz Junior came into F1 racing with a very famous motorsport surname. His father, Carlos Sainz, was a double World Rally champion in the early 1990s and is one of the sport's biggest names.

Now in his sixties, Sainz Senior is still a fierce competitor in long-distance endurance rallying, where they compete eight hours a day for three weeks in deserts and forests.

But Carlos Junior always had his sights set on reaching the top level of the Formula 1 world. He is one of the few drivers on the grid who didn't come to it via the Formula 2 championship and instead was the champion of a series called the World Series by Renault, which was a category similar to F2 racing in 2014.

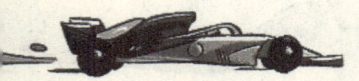

At the end of that season, he was signed up to Red Bull's junior team and paired with Max Verstappen.

Carlos then went to Renault for one full season before moving to McLaren for two years, scoring podium finishes but no victories. His big break came when he joined Ferrari for the 2021 season, and at the British Grand Prix in 2022 he had a perfect weekend, taking pole position and his first ever race victory.

Away from the track, Sainz is a prolific golfer and is often found out on the driving range or golf courses before the race weekend starts.

BEST EVER RACE

In the 2023 season, the Red Bull Racing team were only beaten once and that was at the Singapore Grand Prix where Sainz triumphed for Ferrari. He took pole position and despite being chased down by Norris, Russell and Hamilton, he didn't put a foot wrong and drove to a brilliant victory.

DANIEL RICCIARDO

The Aussie driver is a huge personality on the track. He always has a big smile, but underneath the friendly exterior he is a fierce competitor and a very fast racing driver.

Daniel was in the Red Bull Academy as a teenager and arrived in Formula 1 racing as the next big Australian star. After a brief period at Hispania Racing, he moved to the Toro Rosso team for two seasons before being drafted into the main Red Bull Racing team in 2014. He was paired up with Sebastian Vettel, who had just won the previous four World Championships and was naturally expected to be the team's lead driver – but Ricciardo managed to beat his much more established teammate in their first season together. He ended the year with three race victories and third in the Drivers' Championship standings. He stayed with the Red Bull team until the end of 2018, winning four more races. Then Daniel got a new teammate, a young hotshot called Max Verstappen who was clearly destined for greatness.

In the summer break of the 2018 season, Daniel made the surprise decision to leave Red Bull Racing and join the Renault team, who had not won a race in five years. This was a very strange decision as he was leaving a much stronger team, but Daniel wanted to be the number one driver and he couldn't do that at Red Bull. Ultimately, despite two podium finishes, it wasn't a move that paid off, and in 2020 Ricciardo moved to McLaren.

The Renault move had kept him in the running for the top six places, but for some strange reason, Ricciardo's time at McLaren turned into a complete disaster. He really didn't gel with the car (each team's car is slightly different) and try as he might, he wasn't getting on the podium. Then after Lewis and Max crashed into each other in a race in Monza, Italy in 2021,

Daniel seized the lead and won. It was a brilliant moment but unfortunately still left him in eleventh position in the championship, meaning McLaren no longer wanted him on their team.

Daniel took a few months away from F1 racing but ended up coming back when he signed up with Red Bull Racing again. He was initially a reserve driver for the team but by mid-season, he was placed with Alpha Tauri (the Red Bull junior team that used to be called Toro Rosso) and did such a good job to elevate the team's performances towards the end of 2023 that he earned a full-time seat with the team for 2024.

Halfway through 2024, his career rollercoaster took another dive when he was replaced by Liam Lawson, which means once again Daniel is on the sidelines, having some time off. I wonder if we'll see him return with another team in the future?

BEST EVER RACE

Daniel was in a commanding position during the 2018 Monaco Grand Prix. After being the fastest in practice and taking pole position, he shot off in the lead, but there was a problem with the hybrid system on his car which cost him a lot of power and affected the car's braking performance.

Two years earlier in 2016 he was leading and lost the win due to a terrible pit stop. He began thinking he was cursed, but amazingly this time around he managed to hold off the pack and take victory at the most iconic F1 venue.

BEST KNOWN RACE

Daniel was in a commanding position during the 2016 Monaco Grand Prix. After being the fastest in practice and taking pole position he set off in the lead. But there was a problem with the hybrid system on his car, which cost him a lot of power and affected the cars brief a partial make a

Two years earlier in 2014 he was leading and but the win due to a technical slip, he again took the lead. As it turned out, the tip he crossed the managed to hold off the pack and take victory at the most famous Grand Prix.

CHAPTER FOUR

BLAST FROM THE PAST

You've met some of the drivers racing on the grid today, but what about the drivers that came before them? There have been many brilliant drivers who have made it to Formula 1 level, but there are eleven drivers who are personal heroes of mine. Let me introduce you to some of the greatest drivers to have ever competed . . .

AYRTON SENNA

Many people think that Senna is the fastest ever Formula 1 driver! He's one of the biggest sport stars to come from Brazil, rivalled only by the footballer Pelé.

He wore an iconic bright yellow helmet and other drivers would swerve out of the way when they saw him coming in their rear-view mirrors. In his ten F1 seasons, he won three World Championships and took an incredible 65 pole positions in 161 Grands Prix.

He was a national hero in Brazil but was tragically killed while leading the San Marino Grand Prix in 1994.

AYRTON SENNA

FROM:
BRAZIL

RACES COMPETED IN:
161

RACE WINS:
41

RACED FOR:
TOLEMAN, LOTUS,
MCLAREN, WILLIAMS

★ ★ ★

MICHAEL SCHUMACHER

FROM:
GERMANY

RACES COMPETED IN:
306

RACE WINS:
91

RACED FOR:
JORDAN, BENETTON,
FERRARI, MERCEDES

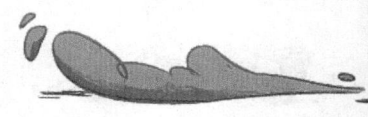

MICHAEL SCHUMACHER

Germany's first world champion was the one everyone wanted to beat in the 1990s and early 2000s.

He won his first two World Championships with Benetton in 1994 and 1995, but then made the shock decision to join the most famous F1 team, Ferrari, for the 1996 season. Ferrari hadn't won a Drivers' World Championship in seventeen years, but Michael worked incredibly hard with his team and ended their drought with a run of five more World Championship wins from 2000 until 2004.

He took some time away from the F1 world but came back after three years to do a final three seasons with Mercedes Benz before retiring from the sport.

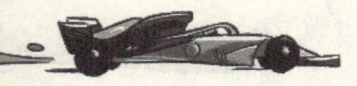

ALAIN PROST

My personal hero was France's first and so far only world champion. Prost's nickname was 'the Professor' as he had a reputation for being technically and tactically brilliant.

He had a very smooth style of driving which tricked a lot of people into thinking he wasn't actually going fast when flying by! He won four World Championships, but more amazingly, between 1983 and 1993, he finished first or second in the Championship in eight out of ten seasons. Prost and Senna were teammates at McLaren and that created one of the most dramatic and controversial rivalries in the history of the sport (read about their rivalry in chapter six).

★ ★ ★
ALAIN PROST

FROM:
FRANCE

RACES COMPETED IN:
199

RACE WINS:
51

RACED FOR:
MCLAREN, RENAULT,
FERRARI, WILLIAMS

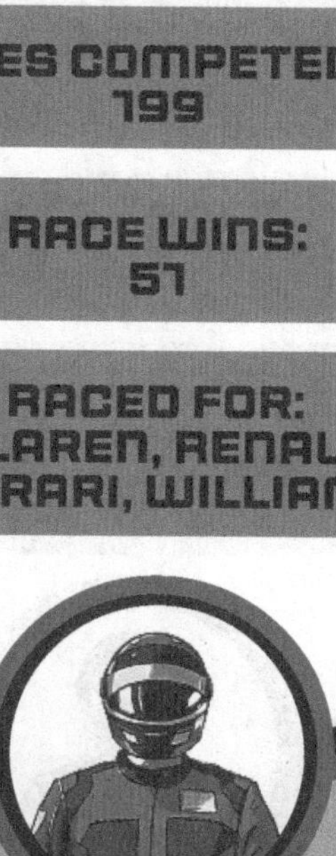

★ ★ ★

SEBASTIAN VETTEL

FROM:
GERMANY

RACES COMPETED IN:
299

RACE WINS:
53

RACED FOR:
BMW SAUBER, TORRO ROSSO,
RED BULL, FERRARI,
ASTON MARTIN

SEBASTIAN VETTEL

Another four-time world champion, Vettel dominated the sport between 2010 and 2013 when he won his four titles in a row, all for the Red Bull Racing team.

He arrived in Formula 1 racing as a teenager with the BMW team before dramatically winning his first race on a very wet day in Italy in 2008 for Toro Rosso. Vettel was mentored by Michael Schumacher and tried to match his hero by moving to the Ferrari team in 2015, but unfortunately he never managed to win a title for them.

Sebastian ended his career with two seasons at Aston Martin as one of the most popular drivers on the grid, retiring at the end of the 2022 season.

NIGEL MANSELL

The Englishman was one of the bravest and strongest F1 drivers ever. Trained as an engineer, Mansell was a tenacious character who fought incredibly hard to make it to the Formula 1 world.

He raced in a golden period of extremely powerful cars with iconic drivers in the 1980s and early 1990s and was a key rival for Alain Prost and Ayrton Senna. Nigel came close to winning the title in 1986, 1987 and 1991, but bad luck struck on all three occasions. Finally, it all came good for him in 1992 when he and his Williams team dominated the season. Nigel became a cult hero across Britain and every time he won the British Grand Prix, the crowd would invade the track and carry him to the podium.

★ ★ ★

NIGEL MANSELL

FROM:
GREAT BRITAIN

RACES COMPETED IN:
187

RACE WINS:
31

RACED FOR:
LOTUS, WILLIAMS,
FERRARI, MCLAREN

★ ★ ★

NIKI LAUDA

FROM:
AUSTRIA

RACES COMPETED IN:
171

RACE WINS:
25

RACED FOR:
BRM, MARCH, FERRARI,
BRABHAM, MCLAREN

NIKI LAUDA

The Austrian was a three-time world champion, winning twice for Ferrari in the 1970s and then for McLaren in 1984.

Niki was an incredibly smart and politically savvy racing driver who knew how to get the team and sponsors working for him in the best way possible. His life was defined by a huge accident in 1976 (you can read about this in chapter six), but he managed to bounce back and win two more World Championships. Niki went on to become an advisor to Ferrari, Jaguar and Mercedes after retiring from driving.

He was also a very good pilot who founded an airline called Lauda Air and later another called Fly Niki, where he would fly the passengers himself. **Imagine an F1 world champion being your pilot!**

JIM CLARK

A farmer from the Scottish Borders, Jim Clark was the best of the best. The fact that he was Ayrton Senna's hero speaks volumes about how highly respected he was. In particular, his racing season in 1965 will probably never be achieved again.

In that one year alone, Clark won his second F1 World Championship, the iconic Indianapolis 500, the French F2 Championship, the Tasman Series and numerous other saloon car races. He built up a special relationship with Colin Chapman, the boss of the Lotus team, and raced his entire career only for Lotus until he was tragically killed after a tyre failure in an F2 race in 1968.

★ ★ ★

JIM CLARK

FROM:
GREAT BRITAIN

RACES COMPETED IN:
72

RACE WINS:
25

RACED FOR:
LOTUS

SIR JACKIE STEWART

FROM:
GREAT BRITAIN

RACES COMPETED IN:
99

RACE WINS:
27

RACED FOR:
MATRA, TYRELL

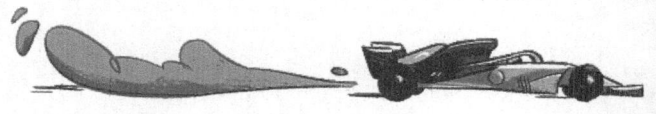

SIR JACKIE STEWART

Another Scottish racer and triple world champion, Jackie Stewart's importance in the sport comes as much from inside the car as outside it. In the early 1970s, Stewart was the top driver in the sport, winning twenty-seven races from just ninety-nine starts before retiring in 1973. But most importantly, Jackie was a huge campaigner for the safety of the drivers, and all racing drivers from the mid-1970s onwards owe him a huge thanks for the work he did to push racetracks and championship organisers to improve safety standards.

Together with his son Paul, he co-founded the Stewart F1 team in 1997 and amazingly won a race just two years later. He later sold the team to Ford.

JUAN MANUEL FANGIO

The 'Maestro' was the driver everyone in the 1950s looked up to as he racked up an astonishing five World Championships between 1951 and 1957.

Very uniquely, Fangio won his championships driving for four different teams - Alfa Romeo, Ferrari, Mercedes Benz and Maserati! He was by far the most admired driver of the 1950s, so much so that he was actually kidnapped in Cuba once! He later said that he was treated well and released safely, but it showed just how famous he was at that time.

★ ★ ★

JUAN MANUEL FANGIO

FROM:
ARGENTINA

RACES COMPETED IN:
51

RACE WINS:
24

RACED FOR:
ALFA ROMEO, FERRARI,
MERCEDES BENZ, MASERATI

119

AND LET'S NOT FORGET THE FULL-SPEED FEMALE DRIVERS . . .

MARIA TERESA DE FILIPPIS

Amazingly, and disappointingly, in Formula 1 history, only two women have officially qualified and started in a Grand Prix. Maria Teresa de Filippis was the first. Maria was the youngest of five children; her parents were an Italian count called Serino Francesco de Filippis and a Spanish noblewoman called Narcisa Anselmi Balaguer Roca de Togores y Ruco y Perpignan (wow, that's a long name!). Back in the 1950s she entered in five races and although she didn't win any of them, it was the first time a female driver had competed on the track, so she's a true trailblazer! At the time, organisers discouraged women from participating in races, but Maria didn't let that stop her and competed in sports-car racing, endurance racing, hill climbs and of course Formula 1 racing. After her team leader, Jean Behra, was accidentally killed in a race in Germany in 1959, Maria quit racing, too devastated to continue.

MARIA TERESA DE FILIPPIS

FROM:
ITALY

RACES COMPETED IN:
3

RACE WINS:
0

RACED FOR:
INDEPENDANT ENTRANT,
SCUDERIA CENTRO SUD

LELLA LOMBARDI

FROM:
ITALY

RACES COMPETED IN:
3

RACE WINS:
0

RACED FOR:
MARCH, WILLIAMS, RAM

LELLA LOMBARDI

It took fifteen years for another woman to qualify for a Grand Prix and like Maria, she too was Italian. Lella Lombardi qualified in twelve Grands Prix in the 1970s and scored half a point at the 1975 Spanish Grand Prix.

Due to a big accident, the race was stopped after just twenty-nine of the seventy-five scheduled laps were completed, while Lella was in sixth place. As it was less than 60% of the full distance, the rules at the time stated that only half the points were awarded.

After nearly seventy-five years of the Formula 1 World Championships, Lella remains the only female driver to have scored any F1 points, with the half point she was awarded in Spain.

Lella fell in love with motor racing at a young age. Despite her father's initial reluctance to support her, she managed to convince him of her ambitions and started racing in domestic Italian championships before moving up to Formula 3 level and then Formula 5000 (which was similar to Formula 2 racing). She eventually got her F1 break in 1974 but didn't manage to qualify for any races. At the opening race in South Africa in 1975, she finally qualified and carried on F1 racing until 1977.

Since then, several drivers including Desiré Wilson, Susie Wolff, Maria de Víllota, Katherine Legge, Tatiana Calderón and Jessica Hawkins have test driven F1 cars, and Giovanna Amati entered races but failed to qualify for the Brabham team. Sadly, none of these drivers have competed in the Formula 1 World Championship races.

But in the past few years, the Formula 1 world has started investing in young female talent. There is a new all-female F1 Academy which is designed to encourage and support young women to become racing-car drivers, and all F1 teams now have young women on their junior driver programmes. I hope it won't be long before we see some of them on the Formula 1 grid!

CHAPTER FIVE

TEAM TALK

When you watch Formula 1 racing on TV, you usually focus on the drivers racing around the track, and when the cameras show the inside of the cockpit, you might have noticed them talking to their team on the radio. But who are the teams behind the cars? Supporting each superstar driver is a team of hundreds of brilliant people who do everything from designing the cars to feeding the drivers. How much do you know about the Formula 1 teams?

FERRARI:
EVERYONE'S FAVOURITE RED CARS

Ferrari are the only team to have competed in Formula 1 racing since the World Championship began in 1950. They are the most successful F1 team, racking up more World Championships and race victories than any other team, and they have the most fans of any team, making them the team that every driver dreams of racing for. You probably recognise them by their iconic red cars and the prancing horse logo called 'Il Cavallino Rampante'.

Not only are they the oldest team in the sport, but did you know that they're the only team to have their own racetrack? That's right, Ferrari have their very own racetrack, called the Fiorano Circuit, just outside their factory in Maranello, Italy. If you ever get to visit the town, you'll probably see fans climbing the fences and trees along the streets of Maranello to catch

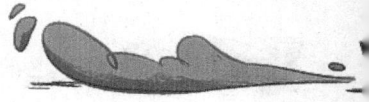

a glimpse of their heroes driving around the Fiorano track. Of course, Ferrari aren't just known for their racing cars but also for their very expensive sports cars. Enzo Ferrari loved all things motor racing and he started the Ferrari road car company as a way to finance the racing team. Today, Ferrari cars are hugely popular around the world and loved by racing-car drivers too – Charles Leclerc has a $1 million Ferrari 488 Pista Spider!

On the track, Ferrari had periods of great success in the 1960s and 1970s, and then the glory years in the 2000s when Michael Schumacher joined the team, but in between they've also had long droughts without winning the title. Schumacher was dearly loved by the 'tifosi', the Italian Ferrari fans. He earned the team five consecutive titles.

After Schumacher retired, the team won just one more title with the popular Finnish driver Kimi Räikkönen. Since then, they have come close with stars like Fernando Alonso, Sebastian

Vettel and Charles Leclerc, who all finished second, but that next title has proven elusive so far.

Despite their last World Championship success being back in 2007, Ferrari have some of the most loyal fans, who turn up at racetracks around the world, covered in red, to support their team.

McLAREN: ENGINEERING EXCELLENCE

McLaren entered the Formula 1 scene in 1966, competing in the World Championship for the first time. As the second oldest team on the circuit, they have something to prove, and with almost 200 F1 race wins under their belt, they're always battling hard with Ferrari.

The team was started by a New Zealander called Bruce McLaren who was an excellent driver as well as a team boss. Sadly, Bruce died in a testing accident at the Goodwood racetrack, but the team continued his legacy, winning world titles in 1974 and 1976.

Then came a big change when a man called Ron Dennis took over in 1980. Ron had started his career as a mechanic and worked his way up to becoming a team boss. Getting the best

engines for his cars, as well as hiring the best engineers, was always a priority. Ron worked very hard and built a very strong team that helped lead McLaren to the success it has today.

Did you know that McLaren were the first team to ever build a full carbon fibre F1 car?! Race cars before the 1980s were generally made of aluminium, but the 1981 McLaren car was the first carbon fibre car to be made out of the same material as a space shuttle! Carbon fibre is a very light material, which made many people think it wasn't very strong, but when McLaren driver John Watson had a huge crash during the 1981 Italian Grand Prix, he walked away without a scratch, proving just how strong the car was. Soon after that, every team had a car made out of carbon fibre.

McLaren have had some great drivers including Niki Lauda, Alain Prost, Ayrton Senna and Mika Häkkinen, who have all won World Championships. McLaren's team principal, Ron Dennis, also mentored Lewis Hamilton throughout his career.

Lewis repaid him by winning his first World Championship for them in 2008.

McLaren are second only to Ferrari in the all-time greatest team list. Did you know that they also have a company making road cars now? This means that they are rivals for Ferrari not just on the track but also in the car dealerships!

After nearly fifty years of red and white or silver cars, McLaren went back to a special 'Papaya Orange' colour for their F1 cars in 2018. This was the original colour used by Bruce McLaren back in the 1960s.

WILLIAMS:
THE HARD-WORKING PRIDE OF BRITAIN

Be prepared to be inspired by the story behind the Williams racing team. Frank Williams was someone who didn't come from a wealthy background. He was deeply passionate about motor racing and dreamt of starting a Formula 1 team. He made this dream a reality by borrowing money wherever he could, sleeping on people's sofas so he didn't have to pay rent and even running his team from a telephone box because he couldn't afford an office! Frank worked incredibly hard to become a team owner, creating the Williams team in 1969. After meeting a brilliant engineer called Patrick Head, the pair transformed the team into a true competitor for the existing teams.

In 1979, the team won their first race, and this was soon followed by World Championship success in 1980 and 1982.

As the owner of the top team in the sport, Frank was able to get the Japanese manufacturer Honda to supply the team with new engines. The engines in this era had 'turbo chargers' which gave them extra power, and the Honda one was miles ahead of their rivals.

But after a car accident in 1986, Frank was paralysed from the neck down, meaning he would never be able to walk, drive a car or even write with a pen again. But he didn't let this stop him from doing what he loved, and he continued to run the Formula 1 team for

the next twenty years – the only physically disabled team principal in the history of the sport! And Frank is still the most successful team boss in F1 history, with nine Constructors' World Championships to his name!

FORMULA FACT

Did you know that Williams is a family business? After Frank stepped down in 2013, his daughter, Claire, took over and ran the team until it was sold to a financial business in 2019. Team Williams is still going strong under new ownership, and they have won nine World Championships as of 2024. Frank's dedication to his team shows you just how far you can go in the sport, no matter what life throws at you.

MERCEDES:
THE SLICK SILVER ARROWS

Mercedes Benz cars are some of the most famous in the world. I'm sure that you've seen a Mercedes car on the road and would recognise its three-pointed star badge on the hood. In the racing world, Mercedes first appeared on the Formula 1 scene way back in 1954. The World Championship was starting to gather momentum and the German car company entered the competition. They were known as the 'Silver Arrows' and won back-to-back World Championships in 1954 and 1955.

The Mercedes team took a break from F1 racing after one of their cars was involved in a big crash at Le Mans in 1955, in which a lot of spectators were sadly killed.

For years, Mercedes didn't compete as a team and instead supplied the engines to other teams, but then in 2010, they re-entered the sport after buying the Brawn GP team that had just won an amazing championship (find out more about this in chapter six).

Their first great move was to convince the legendary Michael Schumacher to come out of retirement and drive for the team alongside Nico Rosberg. With two German drivers behind the wheels of the most famous German cars, this looked like a dream come true, but despite getting some decent results, they weren't able to win the Championship.

That all changed when their new team principal Toto Wolff took over in 2014 and helped Lewis Hamilton to become their star driver. When hybrid engines were introduced to the sport in 2014, with batteries alongside the petrol engines, Mercedes arrived into the new era with the most powerful power units.

This catapulted Mercedes to the top of the Championship, racking up 125 race victories and putting them third on the all-time best team list just behind Ferrari and McLaren. Toto has become one of the sport's most famous and successful team bosses.

FORMULA FACT

Did you know that Toto Wolff is married to Susie Wolff, a former racing driver who was a test driver for the Williams F1 team and runs the all-female F1 Academy series?

RED BULL:
THIS TEAM REALLY HAS WINGS!

You might know Red Bull as an energy drink that adults drink, but did you know it's a racing team too? Red Bull started out as an energy drink that was sold in Thailand in the 1980s, but after a businessman called Dietrich Mateschitz came across it, it became a global phenomenon! Red Bull now sells more than 9 billion cans every year.

Dietrich Mateschitz was a big Formula 1 fan and in 2005 he helped Red Bull to buy the Jaguar F1 team and created Red Bull Racing. Dietrich appointed a young guy called Christian Horner as their team principal, despite him having no experience in Formula 1 racing. But the risk paid off and Christian, working with car designer Adrian Newey, took Red Bull from not-so-serious outsiders to world-title contenders.

FORMULA FACT

Adrian Newey is the greatest F1 car designer ever. He has designed championship-winning cars for Williams, McLaren and Red Bull Racing.

One of their most successful drivers, Sebastian Vettel, won four titles in a row for the team from 2010 to 2013. But when Mercedes launched their hybrid engines in 2014, the winning streak stopped for Red Bull until they had a car and engine that was a match for Mercedes in 2021.

By 2021, the Red Bull team was set for success with the incredibly talented driver Max Verstappen racing for them – he is one of very few drivers who can beat Lewis Hamilton on the grid!

Red Bull had a record-breaking season in 2023 when the team won twenty-one out of the twenty-two races. They're ones to watch!

LOTUS:
THE GREAT INVENTORS

You might not have heard of this team as they stopped competing in 2013, but Lotus used to be one of the most important and successful teams to have competed in Formula 1 racing.

They started in the 1950s when a brilliant engineer called Colin Chapman decided to build racing cars under the name Lotus. His cars were always impressively fast, so other people wanted to buy them, and Lotus soon became a huge racing-car manufacturer that made F1, F2 and F3 cars, as well as cars for other forms of racing in Europe and America.

Lotus officially arrived in the F1 world in 1958 when its first cars took to the track with Graham Hill and Cliff Alison.

The Lotus cars gained a reputation for being incredibly fast but also very fragile, which meant that some drivers didn't want to drive for them, for fear of getting injured. This was a problem for Lotus as they had the fastest cars but couldn't always attract the fastest drivers.

FORMULA FACT

Did you know that race cars used to be painted in the colours of the team founders' national flag?

That is until Lotus came on the scene and introduced sponsors into the sport. Sponsors paid to have their product or logo or colours painted on the cars because it was a brilliant advertising opportunity.

It also meant the racing team had more money to put into developing the cars. This idea was a hit, and now every Formula 1 team has sponsors!

In 1967, Chapman designed a new type of racing car called the Lotus 49 and built it in partnership with the Ford Motor Company and the engine builders at Cosworth. Cosworth were a company who were experts at building high-performance racing engines, so Ford and Lotus pulled them in. The car was groundbreaking as it had been designed with the engine as an integral part of the car rather than something that gets plonked in at the end.

This was the first time a racing car had been designed like this, and every single F1 car has been built this way ever since. Did you know that the Ford Cosworth DFV engine that started in the Lotus 49 is the most successful engine of all time?

It won 155 races across seventeen years!

The Lotus team last won a World Championship in 1978 with Mario Andretti behind the wheel, and although they won some races with Ayrton Senna in the years after, they

never quite rediscovered their glory days. The original team disappeared from Formula 1 racing after the 1994 season, and although they made a return under new ownership in 2010 for a few seasons (for some of which I was the driver!), they never managed to regain the success they had once had and stopped competing altogether in 2013.

CHAPTER SIX

JAW-DROPPING MOMENTS

The thrill of watching Formula 1 racing isn't just about seeing the high-tech cars, their brilliantly fast drivers or the impressive pit stops; it's about those jaw-dropping moments!

Every season has a heart-racing, awe-inspiring moment where you have no idea what will happen next. Here are some of my favourites.

LEWIS VS MAX

The seventy-first season of the F1 World Championship started with a bang! Reigning champion Lewis Hamilton was in a wheel-to-wheel battle with rising star Max Verstappen on the Bahrain track, fighting it out until Lewis secured the win. By the second race at Imola, things were even more heated, with Max squeezing Lewis off the track at the very start.

As the season continued, the rivals started trading blows. No other driver could keep up with the pace these two were setting! It was clear that this season was going to be a two-way fight for the championship, and sure enough, they won eighteen of the twenty-two races between them.

It all came to a head at the British Grand Prix in Silverstone. At the incredibly high-speed Copse Corner on the opening lap,

Lewis thought he had enough space to overtake Max, but the two cars collided, sending Max into the wall at 260 kilometres per hour! While Max and his car were out of the race, Lewis was able to recover from the crash and win despite a penalty for his part in the accident.

The Lewis vs Max rivalry went from bad to worse! At the next race in Hungary, Hamilton's teammate Valtteri Bottas made a mistake and crashed into both of the Red Bull cars.

As if that wasn't bad enough, the next few races were full of drama between the two drivers:

- **A crash in Italy saw Max's car end up on top of Lewis's. The wheel of Max's car hit Lewis on the head – but fortunately, Lewis was able to get out with no injuries.**

- Lewis was excluded from Qualifying in Brazil because his rear wing was found to be illegal by just 0.2 millimetres. This meant he started the race in last place but managed to recover to fifth place in the Sprint race before going on to win the main Grand Prix the next day.

- Max and Lewis battled wheel to wheel in Saudi Arabia. On a fast and narrow track between concrete walls, they were squeezing each other towards the walls at nearly 300 kilometres per hour, but Lewis snuck ahead to win.

By the time the final round in Abu Dhabi came about, both drivers were equal on points. This was only the second time in F1 history that this had happened – the first time was in 1972 – and it was a winner-takes-all finale. Around 108 million viewers tuned in to watch the race.

Hamilton took an early lead in the race and looked set to make history by becoming the first driver to ever win eight World Championships. But on lap fifty-three, with just five laps of the track remaining, the Williams driver Nicholas Latifi crashed and the race turned on its head. When a crash happens, the Safety Car is sometimes sent on to the track to slow the drivers down while the damaged car is cleared away. This could also be an opportunity for drivers to pit for new tyres without losing much time.

Lewis stayed on the track while Max went to the pit for fresh tyres. This meant once the wreckage was cleared, Max was ready to chase down Lewis. However, there were five cars in between Lewis and Max on track which were a full lap behind the leaders in the race. Normally, any cars that are a lap behind the leaders would all be allowed to unlap themselves and join the back of the queue, but with time ticking, everyone assumed that those cars would stay in place, making it difficult for Max to regain a lead because he would have to overtake these five cars first.

The race director made a very unusual and controversial decision to select only the five cars between Lewis and Max to go around and join the back of the crocodile of cars, but not the rest of the lapped cars.

This understandably angered Lewis and his Mercedes team as it gave Max a chance to be directly behind Lewis when the race got going again. On the final lap, Max took the lead with just half a lap to go. Battling a cramp in his leg, he held on to take the race win and title, while a furious Lewis came in second.

THE £1 TEAM

How much do you think it costs to buy a Formula 1 team? One team once sold for only £1 - can you believe it?

The 2008 season did not start well for the Honda F1 team. Their car wasn't as fast as the other teams' cars, and at the end of the year, they decided to withdraw from F1 racing. Not wanting to give up, the Honda F1 team boss Ross Brawn and his business partner Nick Fry offered to buy the F1 team from the Honda car company for £1. It would have cost the Honda Motor Corporation nearly £100 million to shut the team down as they would have had to pay out a huge amount of compensation to the employees and suppliers, so they took the offer and gave the team some money to help them survive for the 2009 season.

The former Honda F1 team became known as the £1 championship-winning team.

The team was re-named Brawn GP, and with a new engine supplied by Mercedes, they were ready to compete.

In preparation for the next season, the rest of the F1 teams had been pounding around tracks all over Europe for weeks and were shocked when Brawn GP showed up for the final test session in Barcelona with British driver Jenson Button in the seat. On his first day, Button did a lap time faster than anyone had done all winter long!

At the opening race of the season in Melbourne, the two Brawn GP cars, driven by Jenson Button and Rubens Barrichello, finished first and second, giving the team a dream debut. Button went on to win six out of the first seven races of the season, with Barrichello winning twice later in the year. Although it was a hard fight against the engineering of the other teams' cars, Button managed to win the Drivers' World Championship while Brawn GP became the first and only team to win the Constructors' World Championship in their debut season.

That was the team's one and only season, as they were bought out by Mercedes Benz afterwards. The £1 team had not just an amazing world title, but also over £120 million from Mercedes!

SECRETS AND SPIES

It's not just the high-speed racing that gets F1 fans' pulses quickening, but also the driver drama. Nothing is as dramatic as when a driver decides to leave their team! The 2007 season started with the sport's biggest star, Michael Schumacher, announcing his retirement from racing. This meant that a spot had opened up on Ferrari's team and McLaren driver Kimi Räikkönen went for it. McLaren's other driver, Juan Pablo Montoya, also left to race in NASCAR in the USA which meant the team were going into a new season with an all-new driver line-up.

Despite winning two World Championships back-to-back in 2005 and 2006, Fernando Alonso made a surprise move from Renault to take one of the spots at McLaren.

At twenty-six years old, and coming off a wave of success, Fernando was unquestionably expected to be the team leader.

But the unexpected happened. The McLaren team signed up rookie driver Lewis Hamilton and he proved to be an equal to Alonso. This was not good news for Alonso, who was far more experienced than Lewis and didn't like being beaten by him.

But it was a very successful season for Hamilton as he finished on the podium in the first nine races, with two victories. Remarkably, he led the points table after the British Grand Prix, which was the halfway point of the season.

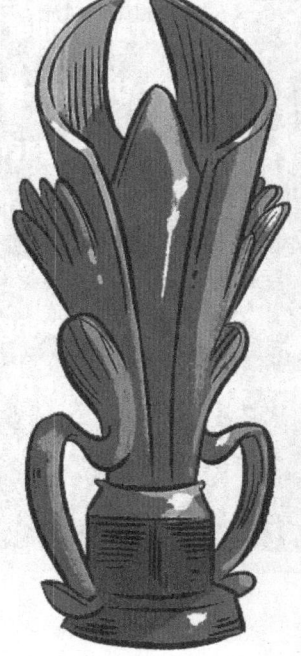

JAW-DROPPING MOMENT!

As if this wasn't enough drama, it was soon revealed that Ferrari's chief mechanic, Nigel Stepney, had been sending the top-secret designs of the Ferrari cars to the chief designer at McLaren, Mike Coughlin! The secret was spilled when Coughlin's wife was caught photocopying the drawings in her local photocopying shop, not knowing that the shop was run by a huge Ferrari fan, who quickly reported it to the Ferrari team! Now that's loyalty to your team!

Back on the track, tensions were rising between Lewis and Alonso when Alonso blocked Lewis in a Qualifying session, meaning Lewis didn't get a chance to do his final lap. Alonso was so annoyed at being beaten by Lewis that he even threatened to tell the sport's regulators, the FIA, that McLaren had the secret drawings of the Ferrari car. The whole situation exploded and McLaren were fined $100 million by the sport's regulators at the FIA. Did you know that this is the biggest ever fine in the history of all sports?

And what about Lewis and Alonso's rivalry? Neither of them won the championship, as Ferrari driver Kimi Räikkönen beat them both in a dramatic final round in Brazil. Lewis and Fernando ended up equal on points, after which Alonso left the team in a huff.

CHANGING LANES

You're at the top of your game, driving better than you ever have. What's your next move? A bid for a Championship win or, for Nico Rosberg, retirement!

Another rival of Lewis Hamilton's, Nico was in a fierce Championship battle with Lewis when he was his teammate. The pair had been rivals since racing go-karts as twelve-year-olds, and Lewis had beaten Nico in the 2014 and 2015 F1 seasons. But that was about to change in 2016. Nico was going for a win!

Nico was so dedicated to winning that he always slept away from his family so he could be well rested, and he ate different meals to them to stick to his strict diet. That's a really big commitment to winning, right?

It all paid off when he beat Lewis to the championship title in the final race . . . But Nico's victory was bittersweet, as only three days later he announced he was retiring from the sport as it had put a lot of pressure on his family. Everyone was shocked, including his team, Mercedes, and Lewis!

I bet he missed having ice cream while he was on that strict diet! Did you know that Nico and his wife, Vivian, have now opened an ice cream shop in Ibiza, where they have a holiday home?

FORMULA FACT

Nico wasn't the only unexpected retirement in F1 history. In fact, the Williams team lost four world champions the year after they each won a championship for the team! First was Nelson Piquet who left in 1987 to join the Lotus team. Following him was Nigel Mansell, who quit Formula 1 racing altogether and moved to the INDYCAR series in America at the end of 1992. Then Alain Prost retired after winning the 1993 championship. Finally, Damon Hill was in the middle of the 1996 season when a magazine published the breaking news that he'd been sacked from the team! They replaced him with a driver called Heinz-Harald Frentzen, who had never even won a race!

But for me, the most confusing driver move in history was in 1976, when World Championship winner Emerson Fittipaldi left McLaren and joined his brother's team, Copersucar. It was a disaster, and he never won another race.

ROMAIN GROJEANS'S LUCKY ESCAPE

Formula 1 racing works really hard to ensure that the drivers are as safe as possible every time they get on the grid, but sometimes all the safety precautions in the world can't prevent an accident. HAAS F1 driver Romain Grosjean found this out first hand.

In the 2020 race in Bahrain, Romain was near the back of the pack, not expecting a podium finish. But when the red lights went out signalling the start of the race, disaster struck! Alpha Tauri driver Daniil Kvyat didn't get his speed up quickly enough and fell back into the pack, forcing the cars behind him to duck and dive out of the way. With limited view in the small mirrors on the side of F1 cars, Romain didn't realise Daniil was alongside him and their cars crashed together. Romain's car sped sharply into the metal barrier on the side of the track. He

hit the barrier at 192 kilometres per hour and ended up going through it! The rear end of the car snapped off and the whole car exploded into a huge fire as the petrol ignited instantly. After the initial shock of the crash, Grosjean realised that he was miraculously still alive. He saw all the flames around him and knew that he had to get out quickly.

FORMULA FACT

Did you know that F1 drivers wear special race suits and underwear that can keep them safe for eleven seconds in a fire of over 600 degrees Celsuis? Pretty amazing!

Romain's left shoe had melted, but he managed to force his foot out of his shoe and then force his way out of the cockpit. It was hard, in between the flames, to work out exactly where he

was, but he found the metal barrier where the F1 doctors were waiting to help him, and everyone was amazed he'd made it out alive.

Romain was saved because the car had a metal frame called a 'halo'. These go from the front of the cockpit and over the drivers' heads. As the car went through the barrier, the halo protected his head from hitting anything, which meant that he stayed conscious and could get himself out.

Grosjean took a while to recover, and while he never took part in F1 racing again, he did race in the American INDYCAR series for a while as well as in sports car racing at Le Mans with Lamborghini.

1997 SEASON

This is my favourite F1 season ever! Six drivers from four different teams won races that year, and nine out of the eleven teams that completed the season all had podium finishes. That never happens!

But the real excitement came from the titanic battle between Williams ace Jacques Villeneuve and Ferrari's Michael Schumacher. The whole season, the two drivers battled for the top spot, but weirdly enough they never stood together on the podium all season long! When one of them won the race, the other was fourth or below; they were never neck and neck.

Off the track, the rivals were quick to wind each other up in interviews. They were enemies in that season and no one else mattered.

When the final race in Spain came about, I gathered my friends for a watch party in India. We all watched with eager anticipation as the race began. Unbelievably, the day before, Villeneuve, Schumacher and the other Williams driver, Heinz-Harald Frentzen, all did exactly the same lap time of 1:21.072 minutes and seconds in Qualifying.

This has never happened before or since!

The grid was set by the order in which they did their laps, with Villeneuve on pole position and Schumacher and Frentzen behind.

It was a brilliant Grand Prix with all drivers getting in the fight. In fact, the Williams team had made a deal with the McLaren drivers to get them to help Jacques win the title. Very sneaky! On lap forty-eight, it all came to a head when Jacques, who was right behind Michael, went for a tiny gap to overtake.

Michael tried to stop him but the cars made contact and his Ferrari ended up stuck in the gravel. The impact knocked Jacques' car too, but it made it across the finish line with its battery hanging on by a tiny wire. Michael got disqualified from that year's championship table as he was deemed responsible for the crash, although he didn't seem to care too much about being disqualified from second place. A bitter end to a brilliant season!

I've shared a lot of stories about rival drivers in this book, but no rivalry was as intense as the one between Alain Prost and Ayrton Senna in the late 1980s and early 1990s.

Their first season racing together for McLaren went quite peacefully, with them winning an incredible fifteen out of the sixteen races – eight for Senna and seven for Prost. Senna achieved his life's ambition of becoming world champion for the first time, but Prost wasn't too disappointed as he had already won two and knew he was capable of competing against Senna. But at the 1989 San Marino Grand Prix, that all changed. The two drivers made a deal that whoever was leading away from the start would not be attacked by their teammate on the opening lap, giving them a chance to lead the pack. Initially Senna led away and everything was fine,

but the race was stopped because of an accident further down the field. When it was re-started, Prost made the better start and led away but Senna attacked him into the first hairpin bend and took the lead, setting himself up for victory.

Prost was raging that Senna had gone back on their deal. He refused to speak to him. They would keep secrets from one another and always looked for any chance to beat one another. It was a very tough time for the McLaren boss Ron Dennis, who had to manage them like two brothers who didn't get along or share things in the same house.

Then, at the penultimate race in Japan, the spark that had ignited earlier in the year exploded! Prost took the lead, but after forty-seven laps, Senna caught up and went to overtake. Not wanting to lose his lead, Prost moved to block him and the two cars collided. Prost got out of his car, upset about the collision, but Senna had other ideas and asked the marshals at the side of the track to push his damaged car back on to the

track. Amazingly, he won the race, but was later disqualified, which meant that Prost became world champion. Senna was very angry!

Prost left McLaren and the pair never drove for the same team again. But they did keep their bitter rivalry throughout their careers, with neck-and-neck races and a high-speed crash at the Japanese Grand Prix once again the following year, which took Prost out of the race and made Senna world champion.

In 1993, Prost retired from F1 racing. In their final race together, they finished first and second, and after six intense years of rivalry, they shook hands and embraced on the podium. The rivalry was over and the two became friends. Unfortunately their friendship was short lived, as the following year, Senna died in an accident in the San Marino Grand Prix. That weekend he had sent a message to Prost on live TV for the world to listen: 'A special hello to my dear friend, Alain. We all miss you, Alain.'

NIKI LAUDA'S AMAZING RECOVERY

At the beginning of the 1976 season, Niki Lauda was on top of the world! He had won his first World Championship the year before and had won five of the opening nine races of the new season. It looked like he was going to take back-to-back titles for his team, Ferrari.

But the tenth round of the season took place at the fearsome Nürburgring circuit, a 20.8-kilometre track in the Ardennes mountains in Germany, which was very dangerous to drive as it was narrow, fast and full of blind corners and elevation changes. Niki had tried to convince the other drivers to boycott the race because it was so dangerous, but the other drivers didn't agree. He decided to drive with them so he wouldn't lose points.

During the second lap of the race, as he approached the 'Bergwerk' corner, he lost control and ended up crashing into a grass bank. The car exploded into a ball of flames and Lauda was trapped inside. Several drivers tried to help him, but it was Arturo Merzario and Brett Lunger who got him out of the burning car.

JAW-DROPPING MOMENT!

Lauda's car was stranded in the middle of the track, and with flames all around, the marshals were understandably afraid to dive in and help. The American Lunger was a Vietnam War veteran and he tried to lift Niki out by his shoulders, but he couldn't get him out as the seatbelt was stuck. Merzario made the unbelievably brave move of diving into the fire to release Niki's seatbelt and miraculously, after three attempts, he managed to free the Austrian from the Ferrari and carry him out to safety.

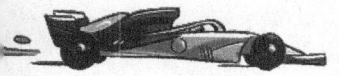

Niki had suffered huge burns to his face, head and hands, and he wasn't well at all. But despite falling into a coma, he survived! Not only that, but he asked to go back to F1 racing!

With bandages all around his head and hands, Lauda was back in the driving seat six weeks later and finished in an incredible fourth place, ahead of his teammates (Ferrari had two other cars in the race as they didn't expect Niki to want to drive again). He didn't win the Championship that year, but he came back to win it in 1977 and 1984. Surely he's had the greatest ever comeback in the whole world of sport!

Wow, that's a lot of drama!

What was your favourite jaw-dropping moment?

CHAPTER SEVEN

BURNING RUBBER

HOW DO YOU BUILD A RACETRACK?

We've got the cars, we've got the drivers, we've got the teams and we've got plenty of excitement. What's missing? The tracks! Formula 1 racing would be nothing without the amazing tracks the drivers race on around the world. But how do you actually build a racetrack? Well, there are two answers to this!

Sometimes, you don't! Some tracks aren't built but use existing roads – these are called street circuits. One of the best examples of this is the street circuit in Monte Carlo, Monaco. This track literally has drivers racing through the streets of the city with spectators seated at a safe distance alongside. Imagine if your home neighbourhood became a racetrack – you could watch the race from your bedroom window!

Putting together a street circuit is very complicated because the designers have to find a way to build the track around the apartment blocks, offices, bus stops, metro stations, fountains,

roundabouts and even sometimes royal palaces! It's always a challenge to create a track that is good for racing but isn't too disruptive for the people who live there.

Or there's the second option: building a permanent track. These tracks must be carefully planned, with not just the track itself to consider but all the extra spaces needed too, like the pit where cars are fixed and tyres are changed, the stands where the spectators sit, and buildings for restaurants, toilets and everything else you need for a massive event. As well as this, the designer has to calculate the distance between the safety barriers and the track, known as the 'run-off areas' to keep spectators and workers safe. It's a HUGE responsibility!

Once the track is roughly designed, the designer creates a simulator version of it, just like the tracks you see on a Formula 1 video game, and they ask drivers like me to try driving a simulated car around the virtual track to test how difficult the corners are, how changes to the height of the road affect the

car and whether the barriers are in the right position. We even practise going in and out of the pit lane to make sure it's right. Once the final design is approved, construction begins. It takes three years to complete a permanent track, but street circuits have to be built in a matter of months! And in places like Monaco or Singapore, the barriers and fences start to be removed within an hour of the race finishing, so the children can get on those streets to go to school on Monday!

FORMULA FACT

At the new Las Vegas street circuit, they kept the roads open during the day as the race was at night. I got to go around the track in a taxi before the F1 drivers drove their cars on it!

THE BEST TRACKS IN THE WORLD

I've been lucky that my driving and television career has taken me to over 100 racetracks around the world. Here are my top seven!

SILVERSTONE, ENGLAND

The home of the British Grand Prix and an incredibly fast circuit that drivers love to drive.

Silverstone used to be an airfield during the Second World War, so it's quite flat and therefore the strong winds can make it very difficult to drive.

The high-speed corners make it one of the best places on the planet to watch an F1 car in all its glory.

TRACK FACT

The first ever Formula 1 World Championship Grand Prix was held at Silverstone in 1950, and King George VI of England was a guest! The 1987 British Grand Prix was this track's most exciting race, as home hero Nigel Mansell got a puncture early on in the race and then hunted down his teammate and great rival Nelson Piquet before dramatically overtaking him with just three laps to go.

The crowd went wild and invaded the track after the race, so Mansell had to leave his Williams car out on the track while the fans carried him on their shoulders!

SPA-FRANCORCHAMPS, BELGIUM

Spa-Francorchamps started out as a street track that connected several villages in the area, but over time, the roads got closed off to the public and it became a permanent track that is a shortened version of the original track from the 1960s.

This amazing track winds its way up steep hills in the mountains, making it extremely fast in the downhill sections. It's a rollercoaster for the drivers, with a 180-degree hairpin (that's a super tight turn!) at the beginning and a really twisty double bend at the finish.

It's an extra-tricky track as the weather is always bonkers in this area. It can go from pelting rain to bright sunshine in just a few minutes, making it hard for the drivers to decide what tyres to use.

TRACK FACT

The 1998 Belgian Grand Prix started with a bang. Literally! There was a huge pile-up of cars. On a very wet day, McLaren's David Coulthard lost control of his car just after the first corner. He was at the front of the pack, so the cars behind him didn't really have much of a chance to avoid it, and in the end, thirteen cars all crashed into each other. Amazingly, all the drivers were absolutely fine, and after a long delay while the track was cleaned up, the race got re-started.

MONZA, ITALY

Known as the 'temple of speed', the Monza track is built around a park just outside Milan. Built in 1922, it is the third oldest track on the planet and has hosted the Formula 1 World Championship for almost every year from 1950 until today.

Monza is the fastest track on the F1 calendar! The cars reach over 360 kilometres per hour (that's three times faster than the speed limit on the motorway!) with lots of long, straight sections to build up speed.

Since it's Ferrari's home country, the Ferrari fan club always turn out in force at Monza and the whole park is normally flooded with the 'tifosi' in a sea of cheering red.

TRACK FACT

The 1971 Italian Grand Prix at Monza remains the closest ever finish in F1 history! In a high-speed chase, British driver Peter Gethin beat Sweden's Ronnie Peterson by just 0.01 of a second, and in fact the first five cars were all within 0.61 of a second. That's faster than the time it would take you to say Monza!

MONACO

The Monaco circuit is one of the best F1 tracks. The circuit winds its way around the narrow streets of the city and you can see the Mediterranean Sea. Monaco is a very expensive place to live, so there are often millionaires watching the race from their yachts in the harbour and having glamourous parties after the race. Instead of a traditional podium, the winners are taken to the royal viewing box and the royal family hand over the trophies, which is extra special for the drivers.

The first race here was in 1929, and it is one of the hardest tracks to drive as the streets are so narrow that the drivers have to concentrate extra-hard when driving through them. The metal barriers are right along the edge of the track, so any small mistake could mean they damage their car – and their team would not be happy if that happened!

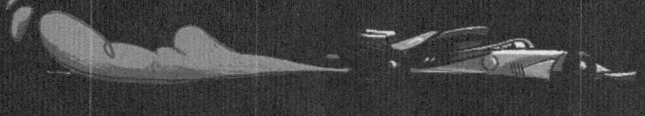

TRACK FACT

The Monaco track is the only one with a tunnel, which runs underneath the Fairmont Hotel. Normally sheltered from the rain water, there was one strange incident in 1981 when the race was delayed because water had leaked down from the hotel after a fire in the kitchen was put out, and it created a puddle in the tunnel below!

SUZUKA, JAPAN

Suzuka is owned by the Honda car company and is an absolute favourite amongst the drivers because of how fast it is and how many changes in elevation it has. The first part of the track, known as the Esses, is especially exciting as it's made up of back-to-back corners that are all interlinked, winding their way uphill and downhill like a snake.

In 2024, the Japanese Grand Prix moved six months earlier from its usual October date to spring, which coincided with cherry blossom season in Japan. Picture pink and purple petals floating down on to the track. The fans are incredibly passionate about Formula 1 racing, and Suzuka even has a theme park full of fun rides attached to the track for them to enjoy!

TRACK FACT

Did you know that Suzuka is the only Formula 1 track with a crossover bridge which gives the circuit a figure of eight sort of shape? Japan is a country where people always try to be creative and innovative with the way they use their space, and this way, the designers managed to get a much longer track without taking up any extra land.

INTERLAGOS, BRAZIL

In the gigantic city of São Paulo, the home of the Brazilian Grand Prix is a really old-school circuit. Interlagos means 'between lakes' in Portuguese, as the track winds its way around the water. Unlike all the other new and shiny tracks on the calendar, this one is a bit bumpy and rough around the edges. It is one of the shortest tracks on the Formula 1 calendar but has amazing views for the fans in the stands.

Like Spa-Francorchamps, the weather can be wild here with sunshine starts and thunderstorm finishes. The roof of the grandstand even blew off in a storm one year!

TRACK FACT

Ayrton Senna was the darling of the Brazilian fans. As a 'São Paulista' who had never won the Brazilian Grand Prix, he was desperate to deliver for his home crowd, and in 1991 it looked like his dream was going to come true. Senna was leading the race comfortably, but then his gearbox started having issues. He had to drive the final few laps with the car stuck in fifth gear, and the Italian Riccardo Patrese caught up to him quickly. Hanging on to the gear lever, Senna started to struggle with immense cramps, but he miraculously held on to win by just three seconds. He was in so much pain that he had to stop his car just after the finish line. The crowd went wild as Senna finally won in his home country on his eighth attempt.

MARINA BAY, SINGAPORE

The Marina Bay street circuit is one of the newest F1 tracks, built in 2008. As it's so hot in Singapore, the race is held at night, and this was the first track to ever do this! To make sure the drivers can see clearly, there are 1,600 custom-made lights shining over the 5-kilometre circuit. The first time the drivers went speeding around the track, they couldn't believe how good the lights were – the visibility was the same as driving around in the day.

With twenty-three corners, it's one of the hardest tracks for the drivers to get right, as there are lots of places to trip them up. It's also very hot and humid in Singapore even at night, which means that the two-hour Grand Prix is often the most physically demanding race of the year. The drivers will lose about 3 litres of fluid from sweating during the race!

TRACK FACT

The Singapore track runs over the city's metro system, and in one race, the Red Bull Racing driver Mark Webber's car got switched off by a signal sent from the metro train below him, and it ended his race!

Since then, the teams have used special electronic sensors and shields to prevent this from happening again.

FINISH LINE!

Wow! We've just gone through 100 years of motor racing history together, met some of the iconic drivers, explored the impressive global tracks AND learnt everything there is to know about driving really fast!

I hope you've loved reading about the exciting world of Formula 1 racing as much as I've loved writing about it. It is such a one-of-a-kind sport with thousands of people involved, from drivers to engineers, mechanics to accountants, and journalists to truck drivers. What job would you like to do in the Formula 1 world?

Whether you are now dreaming of racing around the track or just can't wait to watch the next Grand Prix on TV, I hope you've enjoyed reading about these incredible racing stories from the fastest sport in the world!

GLOSSARY

Aerodynamics: The way that objects move through air. In F1 terms, it generally means the way that the air flows around the top and bottom surfaces of the race car as the car moves along the track.

Carbon fibre: An extremely strong and light material made from thin filaments of carbon atoms that are stuck together. It is the main material used to make F1 cars.

Downforce: This is when air pushes the car further down to the ground. Parts like the wings and the floor are all designed to help create downforce as the air flows over and under the car.

Drag: When a car generates downforce, it also creates a force called drag, which is when air resistance makes the car slower down the straights.

FIA: The Fédération Internationale de l'Automobile is the world governing body for all motorsport including F1 racing, and it is in charge of making the rules that the teams and drivers have to follow.

Formation lap: Before the start of a race, the drivers all go around the track for a single lap where they have to stick to the starting grid formation, with no overtaking allowed. This allows them to warm up their brakes and tyres for the start of the race.

G-force: In racing terms, this is the increased force of gravity acting on the drivers' bodies because of the high speeds that they're doing around the track.

Grand Prix: A Formula 1 race is also known as a Grand Prix.

Grid: The order in which the drivers line up for the start of the race is known as the starting grid.

INDYCAR: A form of single-seater racing which takes place only in North America.

Marshals: People who work at race tracks to help drivers who have crashed out or have a problem with their cars. They also wave a variety of flags by the side of the track to signal to the drivers, for example if there is oil on the track or another car that's parked in a dangerous place.

NASCAR: An American racing championship for big saloon cars that runs mainly on oval tracks.

Pits: The part of the track where the team garages are based. This is where the mechanics and engineers do their work and where the drivers come into for a pit stop to change tyres during a race.

Pole position: The driver who starts the race from first position on the starting grid is said to be on pole position.

Qualifying: A one-hour session which determines the starting grid for the race based on the time it takes drivers to do one lap of the track. The driver who finishes the lap with the fastest time starts first, while the one with the slowest time starts last.

Race director: The person in charge of managing the race. They determine when it is safe for the field to go racing, communicate with the teams and drivers if there are any issues with the track, and also decide whether incidents need to be investigated for penalties.

Rally: A type of motorsport with modified road cars that takes place not on race tracks but on closed roads, in deserts or in forests. The cars go one by one, and the result is purely based on time, rather than racing wheel to wheel and overtaking each other.

Safety Car: A high-performance road car that's used by the race director as a way to control the speed of the F1 cars. If there is bad weather, an incident or an issue with the track, then the race director will send the Safety Car out on the track and the F1 cars will all follow it around in a queue as they're not allowed to overtake. The Safety Car is a very fast road car but still probably thirty seconds per lap slower than an F1 car.

Session: A period when the cars are allowed on the track, which may be practice, qualifying or the race.

Sprint: A shortened version of the main Grand Prix, typically about one third of the distance.

Team principal: They're the person in charge of the Formula 1 team – the boss!

Turbocharger: A part of a car which forces more air into the engine, creating more power.

ACKNOWLEDGEMENTS

Writing this book has been a very satisfying project but also one that proved to be more challenging than I expected. Explaining the world's most complex sport to its youngest fans was certainly harder than commentating to millions of adults around the world.

I was very fortunate to receive fantastic support from the whole team at Hachette but a special thanks goes out to Helen Archer and Victoria Walsh who held my hand throughout the process, and to the book's designer Pip Grantham-Wright. My thanks also to Anna Martin who first made contact with me and floated the idea of the book which was perfectly timed for when I was keen to share my knowledge of the sport with children other than my own.

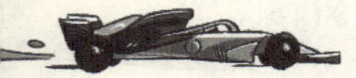

As she has done with her previous children's books, Max Rambaldi has done a wonderful job of bringing my words to life with her illustrations and I sincerely thank her for that.

Growing up in India, I was fortunate to have a mother who ensured that we were educated in a way that meant we had a decent grasp of the English language, alongside Hindi and Tamil which were spoken at home. Sadly, she is no longer alive to read this book, but I thanked her every day when I was trying to string my words together. Her love and unconditional support for letting me follow this career path is something I'll be eternally grateful for.

My father was the backbone of my racing career. He drove my passion for the sport, and without his unwavering support, eternal optimism and pragmatic mindset, I would have probably become an accountant. He helped me to chase my dream and build an unlikely career for a young kid coming from India – a career that has allowed me to inspire others.

The reason for writing this book was to try and share knowledge, stories and insights about this wonderful sport with children. I wouldn't have considered it if my own kids weren't interrogating me every time we watched F1 together, and I have to thank my boys Kushant and Vihaan for their curious minds and for being the 'test track' for me to bounce ideas around for this book.

I firmly believe that everyone, especially those in a public life, needs one person to keep them grounded. I thank my wife, Akshara, who serves as my conscience, holds me to account when I slip up and pushes me to be a better person every single day.

AUTHOR BIO

Karun Chandhok is part of a very exclusive club of only two Indian Formula 1 drivers. Born into a motor racing family where his father, grandfather and even grandmother used to race, Karun was destined for the track and has competed in both the Formula 1 and Formula E series, and the iconic Le Mans 24-hour race. He's been an F1 commentator for five different broadcasters and is currently part of the Sky Sports F1 team which broadcasts to sixty-two countries around the globe.

ILLUSTRATOR BIO

Max Rambaldi is an illustrator who lives in a small town just outside Venice, Italy. Despite being Italian, Max is a vampire when it comes to the sun and prefers to be drawing on screen rather than soaking up the sun outdoors. She loves cats and children's books about science and astronomy.

IF YOU LIKE THIS BOOK, WHY NOT TRY . . .

MATT OLDFIELD

UNBELIEVABLE
FOOTBALL
FIVE-MINUTE
AMAZING TRUE STORIES

ILLUSTRATED BY
OLLIE MANN

MATT OLDFIELD

UNBELIEVABLE
FOOTBALL
THE MOST
INCREDIBLE
TRUE FOOTBALL
STORIES
(YOU NEVER KNEW)

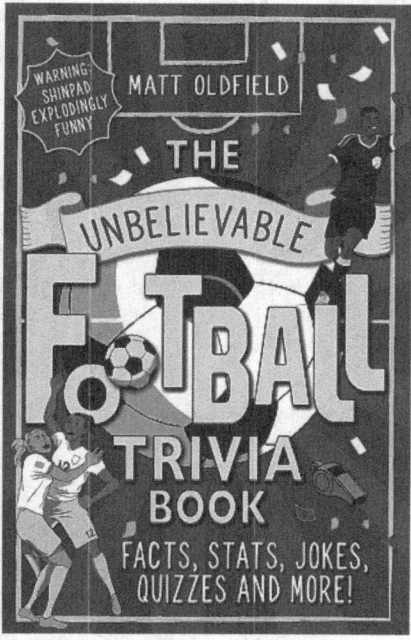

WARNING! SHINPAD EXPLODINGLY FUNNY

MATT OLDFIELD

THE
UNBELIEVABLE
FOOTBALL
TRIVIA
BOOK
FACTS, STATS, JOKES,
QUIZZES AND MORE!

LOOK OUT FOR
MORE IN THE
UNBELIEVABLE
FOOTBALL
SERIES!